EMPIRICAL RESEARCH IN SOCIAL SCIENCES

A GUIDE BOOK FOR RESEARCH SCHOLARS

Prof. P.R. PODUVAL

Director (Retd), School of Management
Studies and former dean, faculty of Social Science,
Cochin University of Science & Technology, Kerala, India

Notion Press

Old No. 38, New No. 6
McNichols Road, Chetpet
Chennai - 600 031

Republished by Notion Press 2019
Copyright © P. Ramachandra Poduval 2019
All Rights Reserved.

ISBN 978-1-64587-731-8

First Edition : July, 2015   Published by : Appissi Offset Printers, Angamaly

Dedication

This academic book is dedicated to my mentor and senior colleague Padmabhooshan Professor (Dr) M.V. PYLEE, founder director of the School of Management Studies and former Vice-Chancellor of Cochin Unviersity, to reflect my respect for his outstanding contributions to management education in Kerala.

ACKNOWLEDGEMENT

This guidebook on Empirical Research in Social Sciences is made possible by my long experience in guidance (formal and informal) to Ph.D. research scholars. Documenting the problems experienced by the research scholars was made by the help of the participants of a research methodology workshop. I take this opportunity to express my thanks to these research scholars and also to Dr. Rajith Kumar, the programme coordinator and to the authorities of the School of Management Studies, Cochin University of Science and Technology.

The book is not a textbook on research methodology; rather, it is on the research process with special focus on the logic of deriving conclusions from data/premises by deductive process of thinking and arriving at scientific generalizations by the inductive process. Conclusions and generalizations are possible only by observations of similarities and differences among selected variables and also by the antecedent - consequent temporal sequence to establish the cause-effect relationships among the variables. Chapters on the logic of research and logic in research, therefore, are very relevant. One may not find much importance to the logic of reasoning in most of the text books on research methodology. This guidebook, I hope, is relevant and significant on this aspect, though the reader may find it more difficult to comprehend and appreciate.

Expression of my gratitude will be incomplete, if I do not mention the names of my colleagues and friends who took pains to read the manuscript for giving their valuable comments for corrections and additions to the text.

Dr. M.V.Pylee, the founder director of the School of Management Studies and former Vice-Chancellor of the Cochin University played significant role in my academic life and as token of gratitude to his role as my mentor I dedicate this book to him. He has read the manuscript and suggested more ideas and also pointed out the corrections to be incorporated in the text.

Dr. N.Unnikrishnan Nair, former Vice-Chancellor of Cochin University of Science and Technology and also a senior professor of statistics, did an extra ordinary work of going through the entire manuscript meticulously even to note down minor errors for necessary corrections. He has shown a special favour by writing the 'Foreword' to this book. To you, my profound thanks, Dr. Unnikrishnan Nair.

Thanks to Dr. M.Bhasi, Director, School of Management Studies, CUSAT, Dr. Rajithkumar, Faulty Member, SMS, CUSAT. Dr. K.T.Jose, former Head of the Department of Mathematics, Bharatamata College, Trikkakara for their help and support in finalizing the manuscript.

Mr. Sreedharan Nair, the owner of Appissi Offset Printers, Ankamali has taken special care in priting and publishing this book. In spite of his busy schedule with other business interests, he accepted the responsibility to show respect to his teacher at his MBA level. Thanks to you.

There are many other colleagues and friends to whom I owe gratitude for their support and help. Of course, the family members are not exceptions. At this culmination stage of my efforts at producing this book, I express my thanks to all.

Kochi-22
18th May 2015   Prof. P. Ramachandra Poduval

FOREWORD

Researchers, especially in the early days of their career, often find several difficulties in carrying out their intended work. For many, the lack of knowledge about the foundations of research methodology and how to practice them have been serious problems. This monograph which is on the foundations on which research methodology has to be built up will be a great revelation to all researchers. Although the title is addressed to social science research, the contents are equally applicable to all disciplines. To my knowledge, the monograph is first of its kind by way of content and depth. The main topics in this work are various kinds of research, analysis of the search part, choice of variables and design and finally the ways of arriving at and presenting conclusions and further generalizations. One of the most attractive features of the book is the logical content that distinguishes confirmatory and exploratory research. Unlike many other treatises on research methodology, this book may not offer an easy-chair reading, specifically the logical content. However, a careful and repeated reading will find it as a unique contribution, compared to the competing literature on research methodology, that will equip the reader with the much needed depth in his/her research work.

Prof. Poduval was my senior in the Cochin University of Science and Technology whom we always looked upon as a great teacher and guide in all our endeavours. I am happy and proud to present this monograph and invite the readers to enjoy reading its contents.

Prof. (Dr.) N. Unnikrishnan Nair
Formerly, Vice - Chancellor
Cochin University of Science and
Technology, Kochi - 682 022.

Kochi - 22
9th September 2014.

CONTENTS

		Page
1.	Dedication :	1
2.	Acknowledgement	3
3.	Forward	5
4.	Contents	7
5.	Chapter I : Introductory	9
6.	Chapter II : Problems experience by Research Scholars	12
7.	Chapter III : Nature, Scope and Types of Research	18
8.	Chapter IV : The Search part (Scholarship) of Research	26
9.	Chapter V : Identifying the topic and specifying it by the Title of the Thesis	31
10.	Chapter VI : Scope oft he Study : Variables and the Research Design	34
11.	Chapter VII : Quantification and Measurement of Variables	41
12.	Chapter VIII : The Logic of (1) deriving conclusions, (2) Arriving at generalizations and (3) Establishing the Cause - Effect Relations	47

13.	Chapter IX :	60
	Fallacies in Reasoning	
14.	Chapter X :	66
	Statistics for Research in Social Sciences	
15.	Chapter XI :	72
	Summary : Steps in an explanatory	
	type Empirical Research in Social Sciences	
16.	References	76
17.	Glossary of Terms	77
18.	Selected Books for Reference on Research	
	Methodology and Statistics	112
19.	Appendices :	
	Appendix 1	121
	Temporal sequence of the variables	
	Appendix 2	123
	Multiple Independent and Dependent Variables	
	Appendix 3	125
	Venn diagram of the four types of propositions	
	Appendix 4	127
	Square of Logical Opposition among the four	
	propositions	
	Appendix 5	129
	Sample size to a given population	
	Subject Index	130

EMPIRICAL RESEARCH IN SOCIAL SCIENCES:
A Guidebook for Research Scholars

CHAPTER I
Introductory

As a research scholar, you have a lot of confusion, anxiety, worry and fear on the research process, especially on the methodology and statistical analyses. This is more so if the nature of the research is empirical and explanatory. The word 'empirical' implies collection of relevant data by your own efforts and their proper analyses for deriving meaningful conclusions by the deductive process and arriving at valid generalizations by the inductive process. The deductive process is for deriving conclusions from certain given statements, premises or data, whereas the inductive process attempts at generalizations from several specific cases observed with reference to a phenomenon. The prime reason for confusion, fear, anxiety, worry etc., is that the research process is unstructured and unfamiliar to you as a beginner to the field. If the entire research process is structured like a PG programme with a limited time frame with the required syllabi, teaching and examinations on various subjects, you are not likely to experience intense confusion and anxiety as you experience now. There is a trend all over the world to structure the research programme, at least some parts as a course work of certain duration. Compulsory course work on research methodology and a paper relevant to the topic of your research is a part of such structuring. But all aspects of a research work cannot be structured as each research thesis is unique in its nature and no uniformity can be prescribed for such unique products. We have to be contented with some uniformity and more diversity.

In earlier days, all efforts in deriving conclusions and making generalizations were the intellectual scholarships of the philosophers as philosophy was considered to be the mother of all knowledge. That tradition still lingers. The academic degree Ph.D. carries the term philosophy whether the subject of study is physical science, social science, biological science, art or humanities. The origin of philosophy is the curiosity and wonder of man to know more and more about everything that he/she had observed in nature. When this enquiry became more and more on less and less in a field of enquiry, we forgot about philosophy as the mother of all knowledge and started thinking that philosophy is another narrow field of study like mathematics, physics, psychology, literature etc. The earlier philosophers were mathematicians, scientists, economists, sociologists, medical men and so on. Their main tool of reasoning was intellectual exercise from their office without taking the facts and figures from the field or the real experiences of people on whom they were making generalizations or arriving at certain conclusions. This limitation of the arm chair speculation of the philosophers was questioned by Francis Bacon (1620; Clarendon Press, 1878) in favour of Empirical enquiry by actual observations of the state of affairs. Empirical means experiential data based enquiry rather than descriptive arm chair-speculations on a particular phenomenon. Conceptual and theoretical research implies the application of logic in the presentation of ideas and viewpoints without providing actual data and their analyses as the required proof for the given conclusions and generalizations. The empirical approach provides sufficient data as the base for the arrived conclusions and generalizations. There are several other approaches too based on different criteria. However, all researches can be classified into four as follows: (1) Descriptive research with facts and figures available by the study of others and also by primary data collected by the researcher himself/herself. Survey type research belongs to this category. (2) Classificatory research has its focus on categorization of the observed phenomena based on similarities and differences. (3) Correlative research is for understanding associations between/among a set of variables. (4) Cause-effect related explanatory research or hypotheses testing research is more complex and it is at the apex level in the hierarchy of the research process.

These four levels of approach in research are not independent and separate. It is in hierarchical order wherein the 4th level includes 3, 2, and 1. The 3rd level includes 2 and 1 and the 2nd level includes 1.

This Guidebook is primarily concerned with the 4th level with focus on cause-effect related hypotheses testing explanatory research. A special chapter on the logic of deriving valid conclusions by deductive logic and arriving at scientific generalizations by inductive process is included. The main objective of this guidebook is an attempt at minimizing the confusions, fears, anxieties and worries of a research scholar. As a prelude to the entire research process, the next chapter starts with the problems experienced by the research scholars in their pursuit of research work.

CHAPTER II
Problems Experienced by the Research Scholars

25 participants in a course on research methodology, organized and conducted by a renowned B-School in Kochi, were requested to write a one page note on the real problems they have experienced as a research scholar—their confusions, fears, anxieties and worries. 18 participants responded to the request and it is assumed that the responses given by them are likely to be repeated by even a larger group. Problems experienced by these research scholars are in two broad categories: (A) problems associated with the external factors and (B) problems associated with the actual research process from the identification of the topic of research to the completion and submission of the thesis.

(A) External environmental factors:

1. Non availability of books and journals.

2. Inadequate support from internet connectivity due to technical reasons.

3.   'Guide is God' and the fear of that God—interpersonal relationship problems between the scholar and the official research guide, based on the fears of the scholar and/or the individual differences in the approach and style of the guide.

4.   Unwanted criticisms and confusions created by others, especially by fellow research scholars without understanding the nature and scope of a specific study.

These external factors that create some problems for the scholar can be solved easily by a change in your own attitude and exclusion of misconceptions on the external support that you expect from your guide and the institution. Common problems are to be solved by collective efforts and individual problems are to be tackled by individual efforts.

Problems associated with the external conditions can be resolved as follows:

1.   Non availability of books and journal: This problem is to be tackled by the individual concerned. You have to take certain positive action in preparing a list of books and journal not available in the department and in the university library after due verification. If some books are already available, look at the references given in such books for further references. Preparation of bibliography on the subject of your research is the first step with due care to take note of the author(s), title of the book, place of publication, publisher and the year of publication. In case it is an article in a journal, make note of the author(s), title of the article, name of the journal, Vol., No., year of publication and the page(s). If you do not give all these details, the Department/ university librarian is helpless to render the demanded services. Purchase of books and journals takes its own time. If it is very urgent, you may request the university librarian to get a copy of the book or article from other sources as it is his/her responsibility to render such services.

The present day technology permits you to get such information from the internet. The problem is not serious, if you do your work in the right spirit thinking that even such work is a part of your research.

2.   Problems relating to computer services in the department: This requires a collective effort to bring the problem to the attention of the departmental head. If it is within his/her resource limitations and control, immediate remedial action is possible; otherwise it will take its own time.

3.   The Guide: It is true that the guide is God to a research scholar under his/her guidance, for you cannot go a step further without the guide's permission and support. The Guide is to be considered as your friend, philosopher and guide and not as a God. Remember that his/her support to you depends on your intellectual curiosity, commitment and enthusiasm and regularity. If you are casual, he will also be casual; If you are committed and enthusiastic, he will also be; you should not be under the assumption that your priority is more important than his priority; he has many other pressing needs like teaching, his own projects and other responsibilities and as such you have to adjust to his priorities and convenience. Dysfunctional assumptions will lead to dysfunctional consequences. Improve your interpersonal relations with him by a positive attitude and enthusiasm in your work.

4.   Criticism by fellow research scholars: Always listen to others, for it could be useful to modify your thinking on some points. But criticism that has no relevance to the scope and methodology of your study is irrelevant. Your study has its own identity and limitations. However, it is better to listen to every one for your own benefits but evaluate such criticisms in the light of your own research design. You respond to the unrealistic criticism without hurting the feelings of such critics.

The above external factors may generate emotional reactions, but, they are only temporary and insignificant. Real serious problems are problems which are related to the research process, especially relating to research design, research methodology and methods, sample size etc. This handbook is more on such problems and issues.

(B).   Research process based internal problems:

1.   No sense of direction in the initial period

2.	Selection of the subject and identification of the topic and title of the thesis.

3.	Criteria for deciding the quality of the topic selected. Is it relevant in terms of its contribution to academics or to practical applications? Is it a researchable topic?

4.	How to overcome confusions arising out of theoretical frame work and absence of conceptual clarity?

5.	How to review available literature without finalizing the research design?

6.	The method of giving references in the text and also listing the references are also not clear.

7.	Relationships among theory, model and hypotheses are not clear.

8.	How to prepare a research design with reference to various variables?

9. Confusions on various variables, such as dependent   variable, independent variable, extraneous variables, confounding variables, moderating variables, mediating variables, intervening variables, etc. Clarifications on the relevance and applications of factor analysis are required.

10. What is an exploratory research and how it is   different from an explanatory research?

11. What is the purpose of a pilot study?

12. How to formulate a hypothesis? Is it required in all research studies in Social Sciences? What are the qualifying criteria for converting a statement into a hypothesis?

13. How to make a problem statement precise and   clear?

14. How to improve the quality of a measuring instrument/test?

15. How to select the appropriate statistical methods for proper and meaningful analyses of data?

16. How to decide the sample size? What are the criteria   for deciding the sample size?

17. Is it essential to use high levels of statistics to impress and improve the standard/quality of the thesis?

18. High level of anxiety on the time constraints in completing the work and also in making presentation of research progress to the full satisfaction of the audience in such seminars.

19. Relevance of my thesis may become redundant when I submit my thesis, though it was relevant when I registered for research. How to overcome such problems?

20. Fear of duplication of my work by others due to my delay in submitting the thesis and fear of duplicating others' work by my ignorance.

21. Worry that my work is not useful to practical applications or to the academic implications.

22. Fear of writing papers for publications.

23. Not very confident in mathematics and statistics and as such the statistical analyses by SPSS, if questioned by someone, it is difficult to give clarifications or correct answers to the questions asked.

24. Fear of evaluation by the examiners. What are the criteria of evaluation of a thesis usually adopted by the examiners?

All the above mental states and sense of inadequacy are natural to any research scholar. Serious research work always contains uncertainty and risk as it is unfamiliar and unstructured. Normally people learn everything by trial and error methods or learning by failures, unless they plan well to get a sense of adequacy. Your familiarity with the research process, research design and methods and methodology will minimize such problems and this book is primarily directed for that purpose.

The problems listed above are to be reclassified into the following three areas:

(A)   Selection of the research topic and the research design:

Problems associated with (1) Review of available literature on the subject. (2) Tentative selection of a topic after review and discussion with the guide. (3) Identification of all variables and categorization of such variables as dependent, independent, extraneous, moderating mediating, and intervening variables. (4) Preparing the research design as a blue print for further research activities. (5) Identifications of the target population and selection of a representative sample and a sub sample from the sample for a pilot study. (6) Preparation of tools for data collection. (7) A pilot study to refine the tools and also for checking data availability and data distribution. (8) Redesigning the research design in the light of data obtained from the pilot study.

(B) Problems relating to (1) the use of parametric or nonparametric statistics based on data distribution obtained from the pilot study. (2) Field work for collection of data from the actual sample. (3) Data analyses by SPSS or other means (4) Interpretations and discussions of conclusions and generalizations.

(C) Problems relating to the presentation of the thesis with special focus on the format, language, style, physical, appearance etc.

The following chapters are on the research process and methodology with special emphasis on the logic of deriving conclusions and arriving at generalizations and some issues on the applications of statistics for research. These chapters are not comprehensive and exhaustive on all details. You have to refer other books on methodology and statistical methods. Books to be referred and glossary of terms used are also given in this guidebook.

CHAPTER III
Nature, Scope and Types of Research

Research is an extension of search in the sense that you are going a step further to the existing knowledge in a specific field of enquiry. It is the process of generating additional knowledge. The existing knowledge is explored by a review of literature on the subject and topic. This part of your effort to be familiar with the existing knowledge makes you a scholar on the subject of your research. You have to read available literature to identify your topic of research and also for providing a background of your study. Research is a further exploration on the subject by your own intellectual work strictly following the logic of reasoning and validating the conclusions and generalisations by empirical data and proper analyses of such data. Broadly all research reports may be categorised into: (1) **Content oriented research** wherein you provide new facts and figures (primary data) in addition to the existing available data (secondary data) and (2) **Process oriented research** wherein you focus your attention on the possible association between two or more variables and their cause-effect connections. The content oriented research need not have any hypotheses, but a process oriented research needs certain hypotheses. The content oriented research may stop at the descriptive, classificatory and correlation levels, for the primary purpose of such a research work is for planning and policy decisions at the micro or macro levels of organizations. The cause-effect hypothesis is a process oriented research for scientific explanation on the relationship between the independent variable and dependant variable on the assumption (hypothesis) that $Y=f(X)$. Most of the descriptive survey type research belongs to the content oriented research. Some of them are process oriented, if they contain statistical applications for identification of similarities and differences of different variables with the hypothesis testing approach. A new area wherein adequate literature is not available primarily due to the fact that enough research has not been carried out so far, is sufficient for you to call you a pioneer in the field that makes your research an exploratory one. Several others may follow you to undertake more and more studies in the area. An explanatory type of research, on the other hand, is exactly the same as described under the process oriented research to establish the cause-effect relation between two variables X and Y: Y as the phenomenon under observation and X as the assumed cause of Y. Other variables associated with the Y are considered as extraneous variables in general with particular names such as moderating variables, mediating variables etc. for their functions in your research.

Research may be classified into several types depending on certain criteria. The methodology that you adopt is the prime concern. If the data collection is from secondary sources and you do the entire work by the use of library facilities, it is a **library type research**. If it is a chronological story of the past in a logical order, then it is a **historical type**. Most of such studies are likely to be descriptive with or without your own interpretations. They are not empirical hypotheses type research. Other types are as follows:

Qualitative Vs Quantitative research: When an attribute of your observations can not be quantified in amount, but cannot be ignored, treat it as a categorical attribute which is basically a qualitative without any numbers and data analysis. Gender, region, religion etc are qualitative attributes. Quantitative implies that the attributes exist and they can be measured. It may also be noted that a qualitative attribute can be made a quantitative measure by an operational definition of the concept of the attribute such as measuring time by the length of a shadow during the day under the sunlight or by the position of a star on the sky. In simple language, operational definition of the concept makes the attribute tangible for observations and measurements. It is also true that a quantitative measurement of an attribute can be made a qualitative one by classifications and categorization and such categories are called categorical variables. The quantitative attributes such as rich, middle class, poor etc are derived from a continuum of annual income of people. In empirical research in social sciences, it is desirable to adopt a quantitative approach than qualitative. Another name for this type of research is **Descriptive Vs analytical or Conceptual Vs Empirical.**

Fundamental Vs Applied Research: Fundamental or Pure research is for understanding the Nature for its own sake for the enhancement of knowledge, whereas applied implies the practical use of the research findings for a particular purpose. Applied research is for solving a problem or for an intellectual support for planning a programme or taking a decision under uncertainty and risk.

Under empirical, there is **Laboratory Vs Field research.** A research under complete control of all quantitative variables by use of several instruments in a laboratory set up is a laboratory or experimental research whereas data collection from the field without any manipulation and control of variables and conditions is the essence of the field studies. One may also call such studies as **observations or participative observations under natural conditions.** A descriptive survey type research comes under such field studies.

Cross sectional Vs Longitudinal research: A research at one point of time inclusive of several sections and variables is a cross sectional whereas a research at different points of time –following the life span of same person at different stages in life—is a longitudinal study. A Study with time series is the essence of longitudinal study whereas a study comparing the phenomenon in different countries at a particular time is cross sectional.

Clinical Vs Experimental research: Clinical is basically a diagnosis for prognosis i.e. individual cases for an in-depth analysis for certain conclusions, but not for generalizations. However, generalizations are possible if several individual cases are taken on a particular phenomenon to observe the commonality among them.

Quantified variables and adoption of the usual methodology are also the essential requirements. Clinical is more descriptive of individual cases whereas experimental is quantitative measurements under controlled conditions. An experiment is observations under controlled conditions. Laboratory research is equivalent to experimental research. Experimental research is for generalizations based on the associations between the independent and dependent variables and not for helping a person after a proper diagnosis. The difference is similar to the difference between a conclusion and a generalization or unique identity Vs commonality. Allport G.W (1962) calls such a difference as 'Nomothetic' Vs 'ideographic 'or common to all Vs unique to one.

Case study research: This is very similar to the clinical type research. Case studies are useful as a teaching method in professional education in business, law, medical and other fields for an in-depth descriptive study of an individual case without much care for generalizations. However, there is scope for generalizations by an inductive process, if there are several such cases on the same phenomenon.

Operations research: It is not a particular type of research, but a term often used in simulated conditions wherein strategic decisions are made by applications of mathematical models. (We may adopt another term for the type of research – **research under simulated conditions).** Such **models** are developed for decisions and implementations of such decisions. Operations Research (OR) became popular during the World War II period when strategic decisions became very important for the military operations. Later, the same approach was adopted in business. In a sense we may call it as a research for problem solving and strategic decision making.

Evaluative Research: If the purpose of your research is an evaluation of a programme or scheme of achievement of the stated objective(s)/goal(s), then you may call it as an evaluative research.

Action Research: When you want to study the impact of certain human actions, design an action programme in a simulated form with clarity on the variables and conditions and later evaluate the programme effectiveness and the variables that contribute to the success or failure of such programmes. An example: How to improve oral communication fluency in English of graduate students of a non English speaking country where the medium of instruction is their mother tongue up to the high school level? Teaching English language by the traditional method is found effective in writing communication, but not the speaking part which is basically a skill rather than knowledge. A researcher is interested to know the effectiveness of a particular method in acquiring the skill of oral communication. The methodology that the researcher adopts is the crucial factor. He plans to select two groups of equal status in their level of communication fluency. Each group has several students. One group is an experimental group and the other is a controlled group. The experimental group adopts a new method of teaching – active participation in group activities with instruction to speak only in English and freedom for giving feedback on the style of speaking by the participants. Models are also used for imitations. The control group, on the other hand undergoes training by the traditional method of teaching by a teacher in English without an active role of the participants. The action part of the research is organizing two such groups for social interactions and the research part is the identification of variables that contribute to the effectiveness of oral communication fluency. It is the social actions and the action learning with the objective of identifying the variables that influence the oral communication fluency that makes it an action research.

Descriptive Survey type Research: As the name implies, it is for conducting a survey for the collection of primary data. Analyses of data depend on the purpose of the study. If the data are only for the purpose of providing information on facts and figures, personal opinions and view points on some issue with some quantitative figures and analyses at percentage and ratio levels, one may call it as a descriptive survey type research. Data collection by a questionnaire and/ or interview with a schedule is always by a survey. It is the purpose and the nature of survey that make a difference in the descriptive type and the cause-effective hypothesis testing type of research. A descriptive type is always a content oriented whereas a hypothesis testing one is a process type. The term 'survey' is only an approach in collecting data. For a survey, a target population and a representative sample are essential. The content oriented study demands a large sample size, of course limited to a minimum as per the finite number of target population. But it need not be so in the process oriented research wherein the basic question is on the relationship between two or more variables and the findings have universal validity. In content oriented research applications of the findings are restricted to the regions and areas of study. However, in process oriented research the sample size has relevance to the extent of avoiding the possibility of type I and type II errors based on the nature and pattern of score distribution. Even a small number shows indication of normal distribution, it is sufficient for the process oriented research.

Whatever is the nature and type of research, all types of research can be classified in four hierarchical levels as follows:

1. Purely descriptive without any quantification.
2. Descriptive and classificatory with some quantifications
3. Descriptive, classificatory and correlative, and
4. Descriptive, classificatory, correlative and explanatory.

All these four levels are in hierarchical order in the sense that No 4 implies 3, 2, and 1; No 3 implies No 2 and 1 and No 2 implies

No 1. The highest is the explanatory type for testing hypothesis wherein you try to establish that Y is a function of X i.e. the Y, the phenomenon under observation (the dependent variable) is the result of the degree variations of X, the assumed cause variable (independent variable), provided all other variables (extraneous variables) are under control. If they are not controllable, the impact of such extraneous variables on the independent and dependent is to be assessed by appropriate statistical methods for deriving conclusions and arriving at generalizations.

Method and Methodology: A distinction is to be made between methods and methodology. Methods are specific procedures and methodology is the general approach that covers the entire research activities. Specific activities are techniques. Methodology is for a particular research as a whole while there are several methods and techniques at different parts of the same research thesis. Research design, in a sense, is the summary of the methodology. Observation method, questionnaire method, statistical methods, etc are for specific requirements. The way to carry out the method is the technique.

Hypothesis, Model and Theory: A theory is an explanation for the occurrence of a phenomenon based on the interconnectedness of several variables in a given context. This is end result of your research which may be supporting an existing theory or rejecting it by your own findings or suggesting some modifications to the current theory. You may even start with a theoretical framework to support or modify or reject it based on your own end result of your research. Theory is the cause(s) of a phenomenon or explanatory concepts and the processes behind a phenomenon. A 'Model' is a mathematical formula for predicting the degree of one variable from the degree of another variable – mathematical relationship between the variables involved and is often used for analysing and predicting the state of affairs of the dependent variable from the degree of independent variable or vice –versa. A hypothesis is an assumed cause (independent variable) for testing whether it is acceptable or not in the light of the data.

Acceptance or rejection is always of the null hypothesis — not the alternate hypothesis. If you say that no relationship exists between X and Y, it is a null hypothesis while the alternate hypothesis or H1 is that that there is such relationship between X and Y. Scientific conclusions and generalizations by statistical analyses are always based on the acceptance or rejection of the null hypothesis and not directly on the alternate hypothesis.

CHAPTER IV
The Search Part (Scholarship) of Research

As a research scholar you are expected to exhibit the complete background information on your subject and topic of your research. As a preliminary work, prepare a comprehensive list of all available books and journal articles and other printed materials on the subject. It is easy to prepare such a list known as bibliography, for one reference leads to others and further references available from subsequent references as a chain reaction. Select some known books/articles for a thorough understanding of basic concepts, theories, variables associated with the phenomenon and methods of your subject of the thesis. This will cover the scope, variables and methods of your research. This preliminary work will give you enough scope in deciding the topic and title of research, after your discussions with your guide and other experts in the field. You should also learn the art of reviewing such articles and books discriminating between what are relevant and what are to be ignored. Sometimes the abstract alone will be sufficient. Focus attention on the views expressed by the author, important concepts, variables, method of study, main findings and generalizations made, criticisms on the limitations etc. Take notes on these aspects and also the full details of the author(s), Title of the book, place of publication, name of the publisher and the year of publication. In the case of article in a journal, a similar procedure is to be adopted, with some modifications such as name of the Journal, Volume, No., year and page(s), in addition to the name of the author(s) and title of the article. If you do not give all the details you may find some problems in giving the references in the text of your thesis and also getting such books and articles by the services rendered by the university librarian.

If you have already a tentative topic for research based on your experience and observations or by listening to the views expressed by your guide or others, explore and clarify idea further by reference to academic material with that framework. Proper direction will be lost when you read all types of books for getting a subject for research without a prior mental framework. After deciding on a tentative topic of research by preliminary review of important books on the subject of your choice, consider all the relevant variables associated with the phenomenon under investigation and then prepare a tentative research design. A research design shows the dependent variable and other variables associated with it and also the independent and its associated variable within a theoretical framework i.e. how these variables are interconnected in a time sequence. Your review of literature is not a onetime affair; it is throughout your research period till you are ready with your first draft of the thesis. It is useful at four stages: at the initial stage for the selection of the topic for research; for writing the introductory chapter; a complete chapter on the review of literature; and at the time of discussing your conclusions and generalization. When you make a declarative statement at any part of your thesis, it should be either an idea borrowed from others or your own statement supported by data from your research. If it is borrowed from others, make it known by giving the reference. If you use the language of others as it was in his/her work, put the sentence or paragraph within quotation with reference including the page(s) number. If you cut and paste the ideas of others without any acknowledgement of the original writer, it is considered as an unethical practice called 'plagiarism', a punishable academic crime. Beware of such unethical practices in the academic world. Any idea taken from others are to be acknowledged, even if you rephrase it in your own language. If you write the idea in a paragraph, show the reference at the end of the paragraph. If the reference is only to a sentence give the reference immediately after sentence; if the name of the author(s) is given in the sentence itself, then show the reference immediately after his/her name. The reference in the text should include the name of the author and the year of publication; if it is a quotation, in addition to the name of the author and year of publication, give the page(s) too. As the title of the book and other details of the publication are not given in the text, all such information are to be given at the end of the thesis in a consolidated form under 'List of references' presented in alphabetical order at the end of the text of the thesis. Page number cannot be given in the consolidated list as the author's name is not repeated in the consolidated reference list and hence the suggestion to refer the page(s) number in the text itself. If the same author has several publications and you have made reference to all, then below the same author, without repeating his name give the reference of his/her other publications details in a chronological order of the year of publications starting from the recent one as the first. If the same author has different publications in the same year again follow the order of the recent one as the first and other publications by marking (a), (b), (c) etc., without repeating the name of the author. What is given in the text as the name of the author, the same is to be given in the consolidated reference; otherwise it will create confusion. Take care of the name of the author: it should start with the surname first followed by the middle name and first name (one's own name). The first name and middle names are often abbreviated to its initial letter. There are variations to this tradition including the form to be given in cases of female authors and also cultural differences. Please read more on this aspect by references to some books on such traditions.

The system of giving references has varied from time to time. What is written above is the system recommended by the American Psychology Association (APA). The Harvard system is almost the same with some minor modifications. The traditional system was numbering at the name of the author and giving footnotes on the same page in the text. This creates a lot of complications by repetition of the same work of an author at several places in the foot note with Latin expressions such as 'ibid', conf., op cite etc. Another form is to consolidate all references in a chapter to be given at the end of the chapter. Often it is called the 'endnotes' or chapter-wise references. Here again there could be unnecessary duplications of the same work in different chapters. The most convenient one is the APA or Harvard System of giving references. Please read more on the method of giving references by reading the list of books given at the end of this book.

Also make a difference between 'References' and 'Bibliography'. A bibliography is a list of all books and articles on a particular subject available all over the world. You may or may not read such books. Only if you have made use of a book and referred it in your text, it becomes a reference. A reference list is different from a bibliography. In bibliography, there are many other books that you have not referred in your work and so it is larger than the reference list. If such a list of bibliography outnumbers the list of reference, there is a possibility of under estimating your scholarship on the subject. If the referred books out number un-referred books in the bibliography, then there is no underestimation and in such cases, there is no harm in giving a list of bibliography with a special mark on those books and articles in the journals referred to in the text. The best strategy is to give only a list of references and not mention any thing about bibliography, and let that list of references be large enough to indicate your scholarship.

There is another problem in giving the references. The ideas and quotations that you make use of could be from secondary sources. You may not read the original work of an author, but got his/her ideas from another author or from a text book. You have acknowledged the work and such acknowledgement cannot be given to another author. How do we tackle the situation? The best policy in such matters is to acknowledge the original author by indicating the source from where you got the information by adding SS (Secondary Source) and giving the details of the publication of the SS to reflect your intellectual honesty.

You may have a mistaken notion that the examiner may not care to read the list of references and sometimes you may be careless in the preparation of the consolidated reference list. The purpose of the consolidated list is to help the examiner to verify the references given and if he/she wanted to verify the authenticity of your statements, they may do so. To be on the safe side, check your references once again. Any reference given in the text should be there in the consolidated list of references and no reference should be there in the list if it is not mentioned in the text. Be careful and take care of such mistakes by your attention to details.

When there are more than two authors, make use of the expression et al. to indicate others as additional authors.
Be careful on 'plagiarism' and be accountable for such acts as it is an unethical practice in research.

CHAPTER V
Identifying your Topic of Research and Specifying it by the Title of your Thesis

No sense of direction is possible without a self perceived goal. What is your goal? – Getting a research degree or preparing a good thesis for the award of a research degree? If your focus is on the quality of your thesis, the research degree is the natural outcome. Therefore, focus on the process and not on the outcome. Taking a research degree is not a goal; it is only a desire. Your goal is preparation of a quality thesis and submission of it within a period of two or three years after official registration in the university. Your goal is to be a tangible goal, not just a desire. To achieve this goal of submitting an excellent thesis, you must attain clarity on the subject and topic of your research. As it is said earlier, problems could be made easy if the research programme is completely structured by making it a course work. In such an eventuality your own risk and uncertainty is low for others will set every aspect structured and familiar. The uniqueness of research is that the work is done by you under conditions of risk and uncertainty. Uniform pattern for all is not possible except in some coursework common to all as in the case of Research Methodology or in certain common background subjects. The goals and processes of activities associated with such course work are set by an external agency and you are required to follow it. The unique part of research – writing the thesis on a topic of your choice—is to be structured by yourself with the help and support of your guide. Even a topic given by your guide is not desirable, for commitment and enthusiasm come out of your own choice and not by imposing some topic by the guide. The guide is only a facilitator of your motivation and not a decision maker. The following steps will help you in identifying and selecting a topic:

Start with a subject area of research in terms of your own post graduate studies, preferably in the area of your electives or specialization at the PG level. It can also be in any area of your choice. Take interest in collecting more and more information by reading relevant books and journal articles. If possible attend seminars and conferences on the subject and discuss your ideas with your guide and experts in the area. Your review of literature on the subject may enable you to identify certain areas where details are missing or area of some controversy where clarity is missing or some gap in theoretical explanations. You need not undertake your own research in an area where everything is clear by the contributions of many authors. Check the titles of Ph.D. theses on the subject of your choice, submitted to different universities. This search part of your research for identification of a suitable topic for research creates some confusion and anxiety as you feel that enough is not enough. In fact you are expected to select a topic at the time of Ph.D. registration as there is a pre-condition of submitting the synopsis of the topic. This requirement assumes that you have already prepared well on the topic of research at your own initiative before the registration by discussing it with some experts including your future guide. Your anxiety on the selection of the topic indicates that you are not very happy on the topic given at the time of registration as you did not spend much time on the selection of the topic. In fact the selection of the topic is very crucial and it may take more than six months to finalise it by reference to the existing knowledge on the subject. Consider your initial synopsis only as an indication of your interest in an area of research and not the final one. The criteria for the selection of an acceptable topic will be clear by your answer to the following questions: (1) is it researchable in terms of availability of data and the width of data distribution for adopting parametric statistical methods? If it is not a known theoretical distribution, you may have to resort to nonparametric statistical methods with less power of discrimination. (2) What is likely to be your own contributions to the world of knowledge (academic or theoretical significance) and/or practical applications? (3) Is it manageable within a period of 2 or 3 years? (4) Are the concepts and variables clear and specific? (5) Is it possible to quantify the variables that you have selected?

Your thesis should not be on a trivial subject or on a complex complicated topic which cannot be managed within a short period of 2 or 3 years. You have to spend more time on the selection of the topic and research design compared with other activities in your research work.

Some may advise you to finalize the topic after reading most of the available literature. This advice leads you to the middle of a sea without any direction. You must have some anchorage or a mental framework when you are reading a particular material. As one guide remarked, one may not marry at all if he is in search of the most beautiful and virtuous bride for him in this world. If you are looking for a topic only after reading all the available literature to make your thesis of an excellent quality, you may never get started. Be pragmatic and realistic. You have to take a decision on the topic within six months after the registration or one year for the selection of the topic and preparation of tools/instruments for data collection. The research design and tools/instruments for data collection and even the topic and title of the thesis may get modified in the light of a pilot study. There are always possibilities for modifications of many things at different stages in the research process.

CHAPTER VI
Scope of the Study: Variables and the Research Design

Once you take a decision on the topic, refine it further by determining the scope of the study. Scope means the total area of your study including the selection of relevant variables associated with both the dependent variable and the independent variable. Variable means an attribute with or without quantitative variations of the attribute. In the strict sense, it is an attribute that varies in quantity. But, in practice, even a qualitative attribute wherein there are no quantitative variations is often called a variable. It is a variable on the basis of differences among different categories of attributes. Qualitative attributes without quantification is often called attributes. If attributes are based on quantitative measurements, then it is a categorical variable. The female/male attribute is a qualitative attribute whereas rich, middle class, poor etc are categorical variables as these categories are derived from variations in the annual income. Age is also qualitative a variable, but when it is classified as infant, child, boy, youth, adult etc. then the labels become categorical variables. Both the qualitative attributes and categorical variables are only for counting on a nominal scale and so they have their own limitations in the statistical treatment of data. Nonparametric statistical treatment is more appropriate in such counting nominal scale. A qualitative attribute can be converted into quantitative one on an ordinal scale. Such attributes can be converted into a quantitative variable by some kind of operational definition of the concept. 'Time' is a qualitative abstract concept, but it is possible to measure in quantitative way by an operational definition of the concept. Direction and the length of the shadow when the sun shines or the position of a star during night etc are indirect measures of time. Your intellect is required for the conversion of a qualitative attribute into a quantitative measure. The difference between categorical attribute/variable and the variable with degree of variations is similar to discrete Vs continuous series. A discrete measure (1.2.3.etc) is a category or a label whereas a continuous series in an ascending or descending order (1st, 2nd,3rd etc) is the usual quantitative variable.

Your review of literature and discussions with your guide and your own observations will help you to prepare a comprehensive list of all variables relevant to the study. Y, the phenomenon under observation or **the Dependent Variable (DV)** is at the focus of your study. Define the concept of this attribute. Do not complicate the study by taking more than one **DV** at a time. However there can be many variables associated with one **DV** as the sub variables or factors within the broad field of **DV**. The same comment is applicable to **Independent Variable (IV)** i.e. only one **IV** at a time and several sub variables or factors associated with the **IV**.

The scope of the study is determined by the objectives, problems, hypotheses and the research design consisting of several variables in addition to **DV** and **IV**. The **IV** is supposed to be the cause and the **DV** is the effect. The cause is always an antecedent condition to the effect. Variables other than the **DV** and the **IV** are **Extraneous Variables (EV)** and they are to be controlled or modified as moderating, mediating or intervening variables.

The temporal sequence of the variables is very important. Any variable antecedent to the **IV** is an extraneous variable and unless they are neutralized, eliminated or controlled, the presence of such a variable is likely to influence the **DV** through the **IV** and so it is to be considered as a **moderating variable**. e. g. previous employment experience of candidates appearing in an employment interview is an antecedent variable compared to candidates fresh from the college. This previous employment experience variable is to be made a moderating variable in the research design, if the effect cannot be controlled or neutralized. So is the case with the **concurrent variable** i.e. the presence of a variable along with the **IV** and such a variable too is a moderating variable. If a variable comes after the **IV**, it has a mediating moderation effect on the **IV** and/or the **DV**. The antecedent variable to **DV**, but after the IV, has also a mediating moderation effect on **DV**. The concurrent variable with **DV** is also a moderating variable to **DV**. If the mediating moderations on **IV** and **DV** together influence the **DV**, then it may be considered as an **intervening variable**.

Variables that are the consequents of **DV** need not be considered as variables of the research design. If you are including such variables in your study, you consider it as a supplementary study with the original **DV** as **IV** and the **consequent variables** of **DV** as the new **DV**. Please do not ignore the temporal positions of the variables while preparing your **research design**.

Examples of different type of variables:

Dependent variable: A particular task performance measured in terms of time taken and errors committed.

Independent variable: A particular method of instruction on how to do it.

Antecedent moderating variable on the IV: Previous experience in doing the same or similar tasks.

Concurrent moderating variable on IV: physical distractions at the time of listening to the instructions.

Mediated moderating variable on IV: nature of engagement after the instruction, but before the task performance, say sleep or some physical or mental activity (specify that variable).

Mediated moderating variable on DV: hunger or no food condition 8 hours before the task performance (DV)

Intervening variable: motivation/interest in the task performance

Concurrent moderating variable on DV: Presence of other people watching the performance of the person.

Consequent variable of DV: Impact of task performance on several other task performances.

As stated earlier, prepare a comprehensive list of all variables that are likely to affect the **DV** and prepare a tentative research design based on the temporal sequence of variables. No definite design can be prepared at this stage as you have no information on the interconnectedness of these variables.

You collect data from a pilot study from a sub-sample of your sample of the targeted population and carry out a factor analysis to identify the homogeneity within each variable, association among several variable (factors) and also associations among different factors (dimensions) by their correlations. Those variables which have associations neither with the **IV** nor with the **DV** are to be excluded from the study. Only if the associations are significant, include them in the study. If you assume that there are two **IVs**, and on analysis you do not find any associations between them, then, exclude one. What is to be retained is on the basis of its correlation with the **DV**. If both **IVs** have significant associations with the **DV**, retain both, for a particular DV may have two different causes, though the two **IVs** are not correlated. What about two **DVs** and one **IV**? Why should one study two mutually exclusive phenomena in a single study? If there is association of a variable with the **DV**, then, it is not a different independent **DV**; it is only a sub-variable of one **DV** and we may measure it for establishing the connection. So is the case with IV. Many variables in a single study makes it complicated, but statistical methods are available (Factor analysis, multi-variate analysis, multi regression analysis etc.). The basic question is not on the number of variables in a single study, but the presence of **multi-independent variables** and **multi- dependent variables** rather than moderating, mediating and intervening variables associated with the IV, DV, or both.

There are many possibilities of having single and multiple **DV**s and **IV**s. They are:

1. The laboratory based **single DV and Single IV** by controlling all the extraneous variables. This is a simple model without any complication, but unrealistic in social sciences as the researcher is unable to neutralize or control the effect of many extraneous variables that affect the **DV**.

1. **One DV and one IV with many sub-variables of DV and IV:** The sub-variable of **DV** and **IV** are not to be treated as separate **DV**s and **IV**s, though there are separate measurements for all. Assume that your dependent variable is the growth of a particular plant. You define the dependent variable as the physical growth in terms of height or length of the plant with the time (number of days) as the independent variable. Other variables associated with **DV** could be the number, shape and colour of the leaves. All these are different measures or sub-variables of the **DV** and not separate dependent variables. If you confine and define 'growth' as the measure of height/length alone, then the influence of other sub-variables on growth is to be controlled by the methodology or redefine 'growth' to include the 'health' of the plant. A completely different **DV** which has nothing to do

with the growth and health of the plant becomes out of place in a particular study. Correlation statistics on association of variables with **DV** will provide the required directions. The same logic is applicable in the case of **IV** too.

3. **More than one IV with one DV:** This may happen, but take care of the correlations among the variables to differentiate between **IV** and sub-variables of **IV**. If a particular variable has association with the assumed **IV**, then the other variable is only a moderating variable and not another **IV**. But, another **IV** can exist, provided that such a variable has significant association with the **DV**, though no association with **IV**. A **DV** can have more than one cause. However, to avoid complications, it is better to make a separate study with the new **IV**, taking into the need for including additional variables associated with the new **IV**. If you plan to include the new **IV** in the same study, do not forget to add additional variables associated with the new **IV**.

4. **One IV and multiple DVs:** Apply the same logic given under 2 and 3 above.

5. **Multiple IVs and Multiple DVs:** Explanations for the non acceptability of this possibility are already given in items 1, 2, 3, and 4 above. However, it is possible to conduct experiments by factorial design for collecting data on all **IVs** and **DVs** simultaneously, as in the case of agricultural research, by variations in the conditions in different plots. Such factorial design is rather difficult in Social Sciences, especially in an empirical hypotheses testing type research. Please note the argument is not against multiple variables in **IV** or **DV** or in both. **The argument is only against the use of multiple IVs and DVs in a particular study.**

Research Design: Interconnectedness of the relevant variables in a temporal sequence is the essence of the research design.

Clarify each concept of the variable and show what leads to what by giving a pictorial presentation. A research design is a blue print of your research activities at different stages and its prime focus in the variables and interconnectedness and time sequence. The temporal sequence in terms of antecedent, concurrent and consequent is very important in redefining the nature of variables as independent, dependent, moderating mediating, and intervening, extraneous, and confounding variables. Each has its own functions. A pictorial model based on the temporal sequence is given in Appendix I.

If your study is not a cause- effect hypothesis type, you may specify the objective(s) in terms of the purpose of your investigation or the problems that you are trying to solve. An objective exists when you have a goal to be achieved; a problem exists when you have observed a difference between a desired condition and the actual condition observed. A statement of hypothesis by itself is sufficient when you are trying to establish the cause- effect relationship between the **DV** and **IV**. All statements are not hypotheses, though a hypothesis is a statement. A statement which assumes that the **DV** is a function of **IV** is a hypothesis. Meaning of the relevant concepts, statement of the hypothesis, target population, sample size, tools and methods for data collection, statistical methods for data analyses, are parts of the research design and methodology and they are the integral parts of the scope of your research study.

CHAPTER VII
Quantification and Measurement of Variables:

"If anything exists, it exists in some amount; if it exists in some amount, it can be measured" (Thorndike, E.L., 1926, p38). This amount for the measurement of an attribute is quantification and it is amenable to statistical analysis and mathematical treatment. It does not exist or it exists may also be expressed by coding in binary digits of 0 and 1. If it does not exist, you may exclude that from your study and if it exists, it is a variable for the study. Even intangible qualitative attributes are amenable to quantifications, if you make it tangible and measureable by an operational definition of the concept as it is done in psychology for the measurement of values, attitude and personality traits.

For measurement of anything we require a scale. There are four types of measurement scales and they differ in terms of mathematical treatment. If the numbers help you only for classification of an observed phenomenon for its identification by a label and nothing else, then it is a **Nominal Scale of measurement.** Qualitative attributes and categorical variables (based on quantifications) are nominal measurements with discrete numbers like 1 ,2, 3, 4, etc. Categorical variables are derived from continuous series, but treated as categories by clustering into some kind of classifications like child, adolescent, adult etc from the age distribution of continuous series. All continuous series are in an ascending or descending order. The position of a particular number may be described as the first, second, third, fourth and so on. This is the **Ordinal Scale of measurement.** Ordinal scale indicates the relative position of an item with reference to all other items in a set. It is a more or less position in a continuous series of numbers. The main defect of this ordinal scale is that the distance among the rank positions are not equal. The distance between the 1ˢᵗ rank and the 2ⁿᵈ rank may not be equal to the distance between the 2ⁿᵈ rank and the 3ʳᵈ rank. This defect can be corrected by converting the ordinal scale into an **interval scale of measurement** by making the distance of adjacent ranks equal on the assumption of a normal distribution of the scores with its **Mean** and **Standard Deviations**. The **z-scores** with 0 at the mean and minus and plus on either side is one method. To avoid this 0 position in the middle, you can convert the z-score distribution into a T-score distribution with 10z as a constant with 50 at the middle. But this T-score may not show the full width of the scale from 0 to 100 and so some others have suggested 14z as the constant instead of 10z.

The defect with the interval scale is that ratios for comparisons are not possible as there is no absolute zero point at the starting point. Presence of an absolute zero point at the starting point in an in interval scale makes it a **Ratio Scale** A scale with an absolute zero point is there for the measurement of physical attributes such as height, weight, length etc. But in social sciences, ratio scales of measurement are practically absent. Quantification and statistical treatment in social sciences are to be confined to nominal, ordinal and interval scales of measurements.

Quantifications of tests/instruments used for data collection: When the respondents to a test/instrument are giving their responses in terms of Agree/Disagree or Yes/No or True/False, the score attaches to the statements are 1/0. If there are 10 such statements, the score range is 0 to 10. It may even have a short range from 3 to 7 indicating exclusion of extreme scores. Any score range is amenable to the conversion of the scale from nominal to ordinal or interval scales depending on the score distribution. The responses may also be in the form of a rating scale such as strongly agree/Agree/neither agree nor disagree/ disagree/strongly disagree with numerical score from 1 to 5. If there are 10 statements, the minimum score is 10 and the maximum 50. Here also a scale of ordinal or interval type can be prepared by following certain procedure. It is not the scale as such but other criteria that are more important such as the discrimination value of each statement, homogeneity of the items, reliability and validity. Care should be taken in the construction of test/instrument on several aspects—concept clarification, collection of test items/statements, selection of the items by its difficulty levels and discrimination index (item analysis method), standardization process for interpretation of the raw score, reliability and validity. Excluding the standardized psychological tests, scales for the measurements of attitudes and related matters are described below:

1.   **Thurstone's equal appearing interval scale** for the measurement of attitude towards a psychological object i.e. attitude towards religion/church /a political issue etc. Collect a large number of statements and process them by using a number of judges with the instruction as follows:

Assume that a respondent to these statements is agreeing to all these given statements. As a judge how will you assess his/her attitude towards a psychological object under the study? The psychological object could be anything that you want to study such as attitude towards religion, war, status of women in a given society etc. Sort the given statements (printed on separate cards) in three bins with the labels (1) Positive attitude (2) neutral attitude and (3) Negative attitude. After this initial sorting, go to the next step of sorting all the negative attitude statement into strongly negative and negative attitude The next stage is sorting of the positive attitude into strongly positive and positive. Statements which do not reflect positive or negative attitude may be put under 'Neutral'. A second chance is also given to make any modifications to the earlier sorting made by the judge. Now we have a bipolar scale of equally appearing interval scale strongly negative /negative/neutral/positive/strongly positive. There are possibilities of wide variations among the judges and at the next stage work out the variations among the judges and reject those items with wide variations by using statistical methods. And the final selected items are arranged on a 5 point scale. This is a bipolar scale ranging from extreme negative attitude to extreme positive attitude with a neutral point. If the scale is made from low positive to high positive, then it becomes a unipolar scale. If it is from low negative to high negative, it is also another unipolar scale. For the construction of Thurston type scale, there is no need to get the responses from the respondents; only 10 to 15 judges are sufficient for the construction of the scale.

2.   Likert's type scale (Likert R, 1932):   Likert-type summated scale does not make use of judges to evaluate the level of the attribute, but uses the data given by respondents themselves. The responses are in the form of strongly disagree/ disagree/neutral/agree/strongly agree against each statement. After taking the total score, two groups are made: Top 25% and bottom 25% of the total respondents prepared on the basis of the ascending or descending order of the obtained scores. These two known groups are used for checking the discriminations value of each statement and those statements having poor discrimination values are excluded from the scale. e.g. The scale values of each statement ranges from 1 to 5 and if there are 20 such statements, the total score will range from 20 to 100 and it is from this total score the two extreme groups of top 25% and bottom 25% are formed for finding out the discriminating statements. It may be noted that this scale is only an ordinal type and not an interval type. Self consistency of the attributes/ statements can be checked by statistical methods such as Chronbach's Alpha test and response consistency by test-retest, alternative forms or split half methods.

3.   Guttmann's scalogram analysis known as Cumulative scale is another approach in the scale construction (Guttmann,L.

1950). In this approach, the statements are condensed to a short form by exclusion of duplications of statements and the final list of statements are arranged in such a manner that acceptance of a statement having a value of 3 on a scale of 5 implies acceptance of all values below the level of three. The total 5 statements itself is the final result of reduction from a large number of statements. Several methods are used for such reductions: elimination on the basis of language, inconsistency, poor discrimination values, duplication in meaning, duplications of the scale value etc. The final selection of statement may vary to a small number in a descending order from most positive to least positive as the Guttmann scale is uni-polar and not bipolar. In a 5 point rating scale value maximum is 5, but if it is a 10 point rating scale the final scale may contain a maximum score of 10. Thus acceptance of one statement is sufficient to indicate the level of attitude of the respondent as each statement has a cumulative value ranging from 1 to 5 or 1 to 10 depending on the rating scale adopted. The scale is unipolar and there are some complications in the procedure of the scale construction. Read more on these types of scales by reference to other books on the procedure and interpretations of such scales.

Homogeneity of the attribute measured is an important issue and so you may have to resort to factor analysis technique to identify the factors that contribute to the attribute or variables. This is so not only in scale constructions, but also in deciding the variables in your research design. A scale may have several sub sections to measure different aspects and hence this recommendation on the application of factor analysis technique. **Relevance of a pilot study:** You may have to revise many things at different stages in the research process, especially when you cannot proceed further because of a mistake done earlier. To avoid such despair, it is better and safe to conduct a pilot study using a small sample of the main sample. If the small sample shows some problems on the availability of the required data, you are stuck at this stage and to proceed further you may have to revise your design or if you find that the distribution pattern is not normal, you are blocked in using the parametric statistics. Your tools for data collection may be defective in getting the real data that you want by defective communication to the respondents. Even for refining the research design some kind of revision may be required and without some data you may not be able to do all these. Pilot study helps you to avoid all such problems with certain data available to recheck your original design and methods. After the pilot study for rechecking everything, you may proceed towards data collection from the actual sample that you have selected.

CHAPTER VIII

The Logic of (1) Deriving Conclusions, (2) Arriving at Generalizations and (3) Establishing cause-effect relations:

"All crows are black". This a generalization based on observations of all the crows in this world. But, if someone reports the presence of some white crows in his local area, the statement that 'all crows are black' is not true. We have to be satisfied by changing the statement by saying that most of crows are black. In terms of the principle of logic and the science of inductive reasoning, no valid generalization is possible unless the statement is 100%true i.e. the term 'crows' is distributed. Even 99% is undistributed.(However, in social sciences, 99 or 95% distribution is accepted as sufficient to make generalization). The qualifying word 'all' or none implies complete distribution and some/most (not a complete set) implies undistribution. Generalization is always a statement or proposition that is universal with the subject term of the proposition being distributed. Such statements are to be true in terms of the actual facts and figures. Establishing the truthfulness of such statements is a part of your research in addition to certain conclusions you derive from data that you have collected. (See the logic of inductive reasoning given in another section of this book).

Conclusions drawn from a set of data are different from the process of generalization. For deriving conclusion you have to adhere to the logic of deductive reasoning whereas, generalization is based on inductive logic. First we shall deal with conclusions by the deductive process after a brief discussion on the nature of proposition and its structure.

A proposition is a declarative statement. The statement should not be with a question mark or an exclamatory one or a commanding one; it should not be a complex or a compound sentence. Make it simple by avoiding even decorative adjectives and adverbs. There are only two parts of a sentence: **The subject and predicate**. The verb part of the sentence is a part of the predicate and often the function of the verb is to link the subject and predicate. Logicians refer the verb term as the **copula** of the sentence. If a statement is a complex or compound one with a many adjective and adverbs, reduce it to a simple statement to clarify the subject and predicate.

There are two aspects of the **subject** and **predicate** in a proposition/premise/declarative statement: **Connotation** or the idea or meaning expressed by the subject and predicate and **denotation** that is the extent implied by the subject and predicate terms. In the proposition 'All crows are black', the idea expressed by the term 'crows' is the connotation and the word 'all' is the denotation. Some words by it connotation may create some confusion if the terms are interpreted in different ways by different people and to avoid this logicians often resort to use S and P as subject and predicate terms. Another expression of "All crows are black" in such cases is "All Ss are Ps' indicating S as the subject term and P as the predicate term. But, there is no change in the denotations of both. Here, in the given proposition the subject is distributed or universal to include each and every item covered by the subject. The predicate 'Black', on the other hand is undistributed as all the blacks are not crows; only a part of black is covered by crows. It is 'some blacks are crows', not 'all blacks are crows'.

In addition to connotation and denotation, the sentence is expressed as a positive one, not a negative one. If the predicate is attributed to the subject, then it is a positive statement and if it denies the subject, it is a negative one. 'All men are happy' is a positive statement and 'All men are unhappy' is also a positive one as the predicates in both these statements are attributed to the subject. The proposition becomes negative when you write

'All men are not happy' or 'All men are not unhappy'. All men are not happy means 'No men are happy'. 'All men' is distributed and 'happy' is also distributed by the denial and so the meaning is not lost by translating it into 'No men are happy'. Similarly, 'All men are not unhappy' has the same meaning as 'No men are unhappy' without violating the meaning and distribution of the statements. Take care of this special feature of positive and negative statements in logic and avoid confusion based on the meaning of the word. We are likely to assume that unhappiness is the opposite of happiness and the opposite word, therefore is negative. Based on the connotation, denotation, positive and negative features of a proposition, there are four possible propositions: (1) A universal positive wherein the subject is distributed and the predicative is undistributed and positive by the predicate being attributed to the subject. Logicians label such statements as 'A' propositions. (2) Universal negative statements wherein both the subject and predicate are distributed but the predicate being denied to the subject. This is the 'E' propositions in logic. (3) Particular positive statements wherein both the subject and predicate are undistributed and positive by the affirmation of the predicate to the subject. This proposition is called the 'I' proposition and (4) particular negative statement or an 'O' proposition wherein the subject is undistributed, but the predicate is distributed and the predicate is denied to the subject.

Immediate inferences from a proposition by conversion are as follows:

'A' proposition: All crows are black

Conversion (immediate inference): Some blacks are crows

'E' proposition: No crows are black

Conversion (immediate inference): No blacks are crows

'I' proposition: Some crows are blacks

Conversion (immediate inference): Some blacks are crows.

'O' proposition: Some crows are not blacks

No conversion or immediate inference is possible as such inference is likely to violate the denotation of the subject and predicate terms. Such a conversion is illogical and therefore invalid.

(See Appendix—III on the Venn diagrams for making immediate inferences.)

Immediate inference is a deductive process. Another deductive method is syllogistic reasoning wherein you have two propositions linked by a middle term for deriving at a conclusion. In syllogism, the propositions are premises as we assume the statements are assumed to be true for deriving valid conclusions. If the premises are not true, the conclusion will not be true, though it may have logical validity. Checking the truthfulness of a premise by generalization is different from checking the validity of a conclusion wherein the premises are assumed to be true, though in reality it may or may not be true. A generalization could be true or false whereas a conclusion is valid or invalid.

Syllogistic reasoning:

When there are two premises linked by a common term, we can draw a conclusion relating the other two terms, excluding the middle term. One of the requirements in such syllogistic reasoning is that there shall be only three terms of which one is common. The common term is often called the middle term.

E.g.   Premise No (1): All crows are black

Premise No. (2) All blacks are dark.

Therefore the possible valid conclusions are: (a) All crows are dark (b) Some dark (things) are crows (c) Some crows are dark. If you draw a conclusion that all dark things are crows, that conclusion is invalid as you will be committing a logical fallacy called fallacy of illicit Minor.

Explanations: The first premise has two terms – the subject 'crows' and the predicate 'black'. The second premise has two terms – the subject 'black' and the predicate 'dark'. There are only 3 terms as the term black is a common middle term appearing in both premises. If there are four term without a common middle

term, no conclusion is possible. The middle term 'black' is undistributed in the first premise whereas it is distributed in the second. Only if the middle term is distributed at least in one of the premises, a logical conclusion is possible. In the given premises, the middle term 'black' is distributed in the second premise and as such one can draw a conclusion without committing the fallacy of undistributed middle term. The fallacy of undistributed middle occurs when the middle tern is undistributed in both the premises. Now check the invalid conclusion 'all dark (things) are crows'. The subject of this conclusion is dark and the term 'dark' appears in the second premise. A premise which contains the subject of the conclusion is called Minor premise and that premise which contains the predicate of the conclusion is the Major premise. In the conclusion the subject is distributed, but it is not distributed in the concerned premise and hence it commits the fallacy of illicit minor. It is logical to assume that we can come to some from all, but not the reverse of coming to all from some. If two premises are positive you can never come to a negative conclusion. If two premises are particular, you can never come to a conclusion as it will commit the fallacy of undistributed middle. If both premises are negative, no conclusion is possible by the negation of two. If one is positive and the other negative, your conclusion invariably has to be a negative one. None of these fallacies are committed in the two valid conclusions given whereas the fallacy of illicit minor was committed in the invalid conclusion. If the predicate of the conclusion is distributed, but the same term in the concerned premise is undistributed, then it commits the fallacy of illicit major.
Example: All crows are black
      Some birds are not black.
Valid conclusions: Some birds are not crows
  Invalid conclusions: (1) No birds are crows.
      ,,   (2) No crows are birds
      ,,   (3) Some crows are not birds

The subject term 'birds' in the invalid conclusion under (1) above is distributed whereas the same term in the second premise for deriving the conclusion is undistributed, committing the **fallacy of Illicit Minor.** In the invalid conclusion under (2) above, the predicate 'birds' is distributed whereas the same terms in the second premise is undistributed, committing the **fallacy of Illicit Major.** The invalid conclusion under (3) above, commits the **fallacy of Illicit Major** as the predicate of the conclusion is distributed whereas the same term in the second premise is undistributed. The only valid conclusion is: Some birds are not crows. Look at the following syllogistic premises:

(1) All honest people are human beings

(2) Some human beings are intelligent

Therefore: (1) All honest people are intelligent.

        (2) Some intelligent people are honest.

        (3) Some honest people are intelligent.

        (4) All intelligent beings are honest.

All these conclusions are invalid. In fact, no conclusion can be drawn from the two premises, the reason being that any conclusion drawn will commit the **fallacy of undistributed middle.** The middle term 'human beings' is undistributed both in the first premise and in the second premise. The basic principle is that at least in one premise the middle term shall be distributed for a valid conclusion.

In addition to the fallacy of the undistributed middle, fallacy of illicit minor and the fallacy of illicit major, other fallacies in deductive logic are as follows: The fallacy of four terms in two premises. There shall be only three terms of which one is to be a common middle term; the middle term shall not have different meanings resulting in **the fallacy of ambiguous middle term;** No conclusions are possible with two negative premises and if one of the premises happen to be negative, the conclusion should be invariably a negative one. Both premises are to be positive to get a positive conclusion. If one of the premises happened to be a particular one, the conclusion shall be only a particular one and if both the premises are particular, no valid conclusion can be drawn.

Remember that in syllogistic reasoning, the premises are taken for granted that they are true, though in reality they may not be so. Even from such untrue premises you can arrive at valid conclusion. Only if the premises are really true by inductive reasoning, along with a valid conclusion drawn from them, the reasoning is strong; otherwise though the conclusion is logically valid, it is a weak conclusion. The picture is very similar to wrong or cooked up data fed to a SPSS for getting a desired conclusion. In such cases, conclusions are valid in its processing by the computer, but not true as the data (premises) are defective. We must satisfy both, the truthfulness and validity. The premises are concerned with the truthfulness and the conclusions with the validity. In research, we are concerned with truthfulness with logical validity of the derived conclusions.

Another system of deductive logic is the **Abductive logic** or conditional logic or the hypothetico-deductive logic. This method is described as follows: If A, then B. It is A ; therefore it is B. The 'IF' makes the statement conditional; A is the antecedent condition; B is the consequence. If you affirm the antecedent, then you can affirm the consequent; but, if you deny the antecedent, you cannot deny the consequent; If you deny the consequent, you can deny the antecedent, but an affirmation of consequent does not imply the affirmation of the antecedent.
Example: The conditional statement:
If the price of the petroleum products goes up, the prices of the essential commodities will also go up.
(1)   The price of the petroleum has gone up. Therefore the price of the essential commodities has also gone up.
This conclusion is valid; Affirmation of the antecedent results in the affirmation of the consequent

(2)   The price of the petroleum has not gone up. From this denial of the antecedent you cannot come to a conclusion that price of essential commodities has not gone up.

(3)   The price of essential commodities has not gone up implies that the price of the petroleum has also not gone up (By denial of the consequent you can deny the antecedent and the conclusion is valid.

(4)   The price of the essential commodities has gone up. From this do not come to a conclusion that the price of the petroleum has also gone up (Affirmation of the consequent need not result in the affirmation of the antecedent)

Valid conclusion in a conditional reasoning is by the following principles: When you affirm the antecedent, affirm the consequent; when you deny the antecedent, do not deny the consequent; when you deny the consequent, deny the antecedent; when you affirm the consequent, do not affirm the antecedent.

Deductive process is from all to some, where as inductive process is from some to all. From your data, you come to the conclusions and you generalise from a sample to the targeted population. Deduction is from general to specific to test the validity and induction is from specifics to general to test the truthfulness. Both processes are complementary to each other. The next section is on generalization by the inductive process of reasoning.

Inductive Reasoning for generalizations:

Arriving at a general statement that 'all Indians are religious' is the final product of a series of observations on the religiosity of Indians. Who has done such a study and how? We have no idea on such research works. Here and there a large number of people started talking about it and when it became popular, a large number started believing it as true though there is no scientific evidence to prove or disprove the truthfulness of the statement. This process of generalization from a few to all is the essence of myth making as the foundation of belief and convictions. The scientific process of establishing the truth is research. Collection of data from a sample and then checking whether the sample findings are true in the case of the targeted population are the essential steps involved in a scientific generalization.

The four types of statements or propositions mentioned earlier are: (1) The 'A' proposition which is universal positive (2) the universal negative 'E' proposition (3) the particular positive 'I' proposition and (4) the particular negative 'O' proposition. Look at the relationships of all these four categories of propositions in terms of their truthfulness. The relationships could be contradictory, contrary, sub-contrary or subaltern. 'All men are mortal' ('A' statement) is a contradictory statement to 'some men are not mortal' ('O' statement) in the sense that if you accept the statement 'O', you cannot accept the 'A' statement. Similarly is the case with 'E' and 'I' statements. How can one accept the statement that 'some men are immortal' (an 'I' proposition) when you have already accepted that 'No men are immortal' (an 'E' proposition). Acceptance of one results in the rejection of the other. If one is true, the other is to be false and violation of this condition is a contradiction. The relationship between 'A' and 'O' propositions is contradictory; and so is the case between 'E' and 'I' propositions in terms of their truthfulness. If 'All men are mortal' ('A') is accepted as true, how can we accept 'Some men are not mortal' ('O')? Or if 'No men are mortal' ('E'), 'Some men are mortal' ('I') is contradictory in their relationship. Contrary relationship is slightly different from the contradictory. The relationship between 'A' and 'E' is a contrary statement of the truthfulness. If 'All men are mortal' ('A') is true, then 'No men are mortal' is contrary' ('E'), is to be false or vice versa, but if 'A' is false, the 'E' may be true or vice versa. The sub-contrary relationship is between 'I' and 'O' propositions. If 'Some men are mortal' ('I' proposition), is true, then there is nothing wrong in accepting 'Some men are not mortal' ('O' proposition) as true. Similarly is the case in the reverse. Subaltern relationships are from universal positive ('A') to Particular positive ('I') or from universal negative ('E') to particular negative ('O'). In these cases, one can accept the truthfulness of the statements from 'all' to 'some' or from 'none' to 'some not', but not the reverse. 'All men are mortal' implies that 'Some men are mortal' and 'No men are mortal' implies that 'Some men are not mortal'. But 'Some men are mortal' does not imply that 'All men are mortal' and 'Some men are not mortal' does not imply that 'No men are mortal'.

(Appendix—IV gives a pictorial view of these relationships of the basic four propositions with respect to the truthfulness).

The logic of Cause-Effect Relationship:

A correlation between two variables indicates association between them and this association need not be interpreted as the cause-effect relationship, unless the variables are in an antecedent and consequent in temporal sequence. Further explorations are required to make a prediction from the level of one variable to the level of the other variable. This covariance relationship in two or more variables is often made by using regression analysis or multiple regression analyses. A mathematical formula for the prediction can also be made by the use of by some equation model such as the Structural Equation Model (SEM). The rationale behind such cause-effect model is the essence of the logic of inductive process. The theory of causation by Mill (Mill, J.S. 1843) is relevant at this juncture. The basic principles of causations are as follows:

1.   The Method of Agreement:

"If two or more instances of the phenomenon under investigation have only one circumstance in common, the circumstance in which alone all the instances agree, is the cause or effect of the given phenomenon" (Mill, J.S. 1843 p.454).

If 'Y' is the phenomenon under observation or the Dependent Variable (DV), and 'X' is the assumed cause or the Independent Variable (IV), then the presence of X always results in Y and so it is a necessary condition for the presence of Y. But, this does not mean that Y will not occur in the absence of X, for there could be other causes for the presence of Y. In other words, a necessary condition alone is not sufficient for establishing the cause-effect relationship. To make it a strong cause, we must attain a condition of necessary and sufficient cause. Y never occurs in the absence of X is not a corollary in this method of agreement, but whenever X is present Y is also present is a necessary condition for the causation.

2.   The Method of Difference:

"If an instance in which the phenomenon under investigation occurs and an instance in which it does not occur, have every circumstance save one in common, that one occurring only in the former, the circumstance in which alone the two instances differ, is the effect or the cause or a necessary part of the cause of the phenomenon" Mill, J.S. 1843, p.455)

Y occurs in the presence of X and Y does not occur in absence of X. Now X becomes a sufficient cause or at least a part of the cause of Y. A combination of 'the method of agreement' and 'the method of difference' makes 'X' both a necessary and sufficient condition for the establishment of the cause-effect relationship.

3.   The Joint Method of Agreement and Difference:

"If two or more instances in which the phenomenon occurs have only one circumstance in common, while in two or more instances in which it does not occur have nothing in common save the absence of that circumstance, the circumstances in which alone the two sets of instances differ, is the effect or cause or a necessary part of the cause of the phenomenon" (Mill, J.S. 1843, p.463)

This principle of causation is only a combination of (1) and (2) above with focus on both the necessary and sufficient Conditions for the causation.

4.   The Method of Residue:

"Subduct from any phenomenon such part as is known by previous inductions to be the effect of certain antecedent and the residue of that phenomenon is the effect of the remaining antecedents" (Mill, J.S. 1843, p. 465.).

If ABC occurs together with xyz, and B is known to be the cause of y and C is known as the cause of z, then A is the cause or effect of x. You may note the expression 'cause or effect' in most of the principles, not being sure whether it is the cause or effect. This is primarily due to the fact that we are not sure whether it is an antecedent or a consequent in the given circumstances. If X is the antecedent, then it is the cause and if it is the consequent, then it is the effect.

5.   The Method of Concomitant Variations:

In addition to the methods described under (1), (2), (3) and (4) above, Mill speaks about the method of concomitant variations as follows:

Variations in the value of the cause or the independent variable (IV) should result in a corresponding variation in the value of the phenomenon under observation or the dependent variable (DV) either in a positive or its inverse. The co-variations between the two variables are equally important in establishing the cause-effect relationship between two or more variables. There are some statistical methods to ascertain such relationships. According to Mill, "Whatever phenomenon varies in any manner whenever another phenomenon varies in some particular manner, is either the cause or an effect of the phenomenon or is connected with it through some fact of causation" (Mill, J.S. 1843, p.470). From the laws of causation as given by John Stuart Mill, it is clear that what we have to look for are similarities and differences and the degree of associations between IV and DV. The statistical tools that you apply in your research are associated with the measurements of similarities (e.g. correlations), differences (e. g. t-test; ANOVA, MANOVA etc) and co-variations/concomitant variations between two or more variables (regression and multi-regression analyses) to create a mathematical formula for prediction from one variable to the other on the assumption of causation or $Y=f(X)$.

Hypothesis testing research is basically for establishing a cause-effect relationship between Y, the phenomenon under observations and X, the assumed cause of Y. X is the antecedent variable and Y is the consequent variable. In your research design exclude the effects of Y as your study is on Y, the effect of X. If you study the effect of Y, then Y becomes an independent variable to its effect as the dependent variable. But, there is nothing wrong if you study the effect of Y as a supplementary one with a new research design by changing the role of the original Y as a new IV to new DVs.

A note on the null hypothesis (H0) and alternative hypothesis (H1) is relevant in this context. You do not have freedom to change the meaning to suit your convenience. Null hypothesis implies that X is not the cause of Y; there is no difference between X and Y; they are homogeneous or similar rather than different. H1, the alternative hypothesis is the opposite; there is a significant difference; they are not from a homogenous population. Writing a hypothesis in the form of a null hypothesis or writing the null hypothesis in the form of a hypothesis is to be avoided. The real statistical test is only on the null hypothesis and not on hypothesis i.e. the alternative hypothesis. Your acceptance or rejection is not the hypothesis, but on the null hypothesis. Rejection or acceptance of hypothesis is indirect by acceptance or rejection of the null hypothesis. We are sure of the acceptance or rejection of the null hypothesis, but not so sure of the alternative hypothesis and to ensure that rejection or acceptance of the alternative hypothesis, more care is required in the design and methodology of your research study.

CHAPTER IX
Fallacies in Reasoning

(Note: Assume that your thesis is subjected to scrutiny in a Court of Reasoning and there is an expert logician to argue against some contents of your thesis in the form of a statement/ conclusions/generalizations and recommendations. The criticisms could be overcome, if you are aware of the possible fallacies in your arguments)

A fallacy is an error in reasoning by violating the principles of right reasoning. It could be in several forms. (1) Giving recommendations without any reference to the conclusions and generalizations given in the thesis. (2) Generalizations without a sound inductive reasoning (3) Conclusions that do not follow the data analysis and proper interpretations. (4) Statements that are faulty and also without any support from your data or support of findings of other researchers in the field.

Generalizations are more on the truthfulness of a given statement/proposition/premises whereas validity is on the conclusions derived from the data. A statement is either true or false and a conclusion is either valid or invalid. A sound conclusion is both true and valid and weak conclusion though valid is not true or though true, is not valid. The primary concern is the truthfulness of a statement in terms of its reflections of the reality of facts and figures; and the validity of conclusions cannot be ignored. Make it a sound argument by doing justice to both truthfulness and validity.

Fallacies in Deductive Reasoning:

(A)   Fallacies in immediate inference:

1. From 'All men are mortal', do not come to an inference, that 'All mortals are men'. The valid inference is that 'Some mortals

are men'. The first inference violates the principle of distribution of the predicate term. However, no such violation is there, if your inference is 'Some mortals are men'.

2 There is no harm in reversing the order in the case of universal negative or particular positive propositions; such conversions do not violate the principles of distribution. However, the particular negative proposition is not amenable to conversion as it violates the principle of distribution. In such propositions, the conversion results in a distribution of the subject term which is undistributed in the original proposition.

(B)   Fallacies in Syllogistic reasoning:

Coming to a conclusion by linking two premises is the essence of syllogistic reasoning. The possible fallacies are as follows:

1.   Fallacy of four terms in two premises: From two premises without a common middle term, no conclusion can be drawn; there shall be only 3 terms of which one shall be common.

2.   Fallacy of the ambiguous middle term: The middle term may look the same in two premises, but may differ in their meaning that creates confusion in their connotations. Such middle terms if used in ambiguous meanings results in invalid conclusion as no conclusion can be drawn from such premises.

3.   Fallacy of undistributed middle terms: If both premises are undistributed, no valid conclusion can be drawn from the premises; at least one of the premises shall contain a distributed middle term for deriving any conclusion.

4.   Fallacy of two negative premises: No conclusion can be drawn from two negative premises.

5.   Fallacy of two particular premises: If both the premises are particular, no conclusion can be drawn.

6.   Fallacy of drawing positive conclusion from a negative premise: If a negative premise is present in a syllogism, the conclusion shall be negative. Only from two positive premises, one can draw a positive conclusion.

7.   Fallacy of Illicit Minor: If the subject of the conclusion is distributed, the premise that contains the subject term is the Minor

premise and in such a minor premise, the subject term shall be distributed; otherwise it commits the fallacy of illicit Minor.

8.   Fallacy of illicit Major: The premise that contains the predicate of the conclusion is the Major premise. If the predicate of the conclusion is distributed, the same term in the premise shall also be distributed; otherwise, it commits the fallacy of illicit Major.

(C)   Deductive reasoning from conditional abductive logic:

1.   Fallacy of denial of the antecedent for the denial of the consequent: If you affirm the antecedent, affirm the consequent; but if you deny the antecedent, and then deny the consequent, you commit this fallacy. e.g. "If it rains, the soil will be wet"; "It has rained, therefore, the soil is wet". This affirmation of the antecedent results in the affirmation of the consequent and it is a valid conclusion. But, from the statement "there was no rain" do not conclude that "the soil is not wet', for the soil could be wet by other reasons.

2. Fallacy of affirmation of the antecedent by the affirmation of the consequent: By denial of the consequent, one can deny the antecedent; "the soil is not wet", therefore "there was no rain" is a valid conclusion; but to say that "the soil is wet" and therefore "there was rain" is an invalid conclusion as the soil could be wet due to other reasons.

(D) Fallacies in inductive reasoning: From specific instances to a general statement is the essence of generalization. There are many fallacies under this category. Some of them relating to the truthfulness of the statements are listed below:

1. Fallacies in Contradictories: "All men are mortal" is an 'A' proposition(universal positive) and "Some men are not mortal" is an 'O' proposition (Particular negative); Both these statements are contradictory for if the first one is accepted as true, the other one ought to be false or vice versa. One cannot accept both as true; and both cannot be false. Similarly, If "No men are mortal" (a universal negative 'E' proposition) is true, then "Some men are mortal" (particular positive 'I' proposition) is a contradictory

statement; both cannot be true at the same time, and both cannot be false.

2. Fallacies in Contraries: "All men are mortal" ('A' Proposition) and "No men are mortal" ('E' proposition) are contrary statements and not contradictory. Acceptance of the first statement as true results in making the second statement false and vice versa; but if 'A' is false, 'E' is indeterminate for it could be true or false. Similarly, if 'E' is false, 'A' is indeterminate for it could be True of False.

1.   Fallacies in Sub contraries: Sub contraries are two particular propositions, one positive and the other negative e.g. "Some men are mortal" (particular positive 'I' proposition) and "Some men are not mortal" (particular negative 'O' proposition). If 'I' is true, then 'O' is indeterminate of being true or false. If 'O' is true, 'I' is indeterminate of being true or false. 'I' and 'O' both cannot be false; at least, one of them is to be true. If 'I' is false, 'O' is true.

2.   Fallacies in Subaltern (a) Relationship between 'A' proposition and 'I' proposition. If 'A' is true, then 'I' is also true; but if 'I' is true, 'A' may be true or false. But, if 'I' is false 'A" is also false; if 'A' is false then, 'I' is indeterminate of being true or false .

3.   Fallacies of Subaltern (b): Relationship between the 'E' proposition and the 'O' proposition. If 'E' is true, then 'O' is also true, and if 'E' is false, 'O' is also false. But, if 'O' is true, 'E' is indeterminate of being true or false.

6. Fallacy of biased sample: Sample selected does not represent the target population by the method of selection. Convenience sampling, deliberate sampling, judgemental sampling etc are likely to result in such fallacies

7. Fallacy of limited sample: Inadequate sample size creates this fallacy.

(E) Fallacies of convenience for creating confusions and dilemma in the mind of the opponent:

1. Fallacy of unwanted or incomparable analogies: Irrelevant similarities for winning an argument.
2. Fallacy of division: Fallacy arising out of the view that if it is true for the whole, it must be true for all its parts.
3. Fallacy of composition: Fallacy arising out of the view that if it is true for a part, it must be true for the whole.
4. Fallacy of the spot light: exaggeration or misleading vividness of insignificant aspects, ignoring other important aspects.
5. Fallacy of the Straw man: Misrepresented version of a position, a person, or an event.
6. Fallacy of ignoring the intermediate steps and connecting the first with the last
7. Fallacy of making two wrongs as the right one: e.g. My enemy's enemy is my friend.
8. Fallacy of special Pleading by an emotional appeal.
9. Fallacy of Red Herring: Irrelevant topic to side tract the main issue.
10. Fallacy of the questionable cause: Simultaneous occurrence of A and B resulting in a statement that A is the cause of B or B is the cause of A; a co- occurrence or correlation need not be the cause.
11. Fallacy of 'Post Hoc Ergo Propter Hoc': Confusing coincidental relations with cause or simply false cause.
12. Fallacy of poisoning the well: Presenting unfavourable information for spoiling the victory of the other.
13. Fallacy of 'Ad Hominem': Attacking the person who presents a view, instead of discussion of the central issue.
14. Fallacy of the middle ground: If both extremes are not acceptable, preference to the middle of the road views without any reason.
15. Fallacy of ignoring the common cause: An association between two could be the consequence of a third common factor.
16. Fallacy of explaining something with a verbal labelling or by a concept not well explained. Words like inborn, innate, genetic, hereditary, instinct, extra cerebral memory etc are examples.

17. Gamblers' Fallacy: Unrealistic expectations with high risk.
18. Fallacy of Black and White Thinking: Explanation by categorizations; extreme views by ignoring the full view of an issue.
19. Fallacy of 'Ad ignoratium': Appeal to ignorance; putting the burden of proof to the opposite party.
20. Fallacy of 'Petitio Principii': Begging the question or reasoning in circle.
21. Fallacy of 'Bandwagon': Joining with the peer group or succumbing to the pressure of the peer group to avoid isolation and rejection.
22. Fallacy of appeal to non issues resorted to by many: Appeal to emotions, beliefs and convictions such as appeal to celebrity, appeal to flattery, appeal to traditions, appeal to novelty, appeal to pity, appeal to popularity, appeal to 'practical', appeal to common practices, appeal to authority, appeal to beliefs etc.
23. Relativistic or subjective Fallacies: Generalizations from subjective experiences and generalizations from exceptions.

CHAPTER X
Statistics for Research in Social Sciences

Statistics is an academic discipline that deals with numerical information called 'Data' and quantifications by different scales of measurements. It is a mathematical science, but not a branch of mathematics for data collection, data interpretation and applications of several methods for making inferences on the similarities, differences and co-variations of different sets of data (variables). The broad field of statistics is sub-divided into parametric on the assumption of probability distribution and nonparametric on the assumption of distribution free data. A further subdivision is descriptive Vs inferential statistics. Descriptive statistics provides a picture of the state of affairs on the representative of the whole in terms of the central values (mean, median and mode), and variations of data distribution of the entire sample/population in the forms of mean deviation, standard deviation, quartile deviation, etc and also range and variance. The descriptive statistics enables one to come to certain conclusions by the deductive process. The second category of inferential statistics is helpful to arrive at certain generalizations from sample to its population. Conclusions are often made by the deductive logic whereas generalizations are made by the inductive methods.

Whether you have to adopt parametric or nonparametric method is to be decided on the basis of the nature of the data obtained in your research. If the distribution pattern is in tune with the normal probability distribution, adopt parametric statistical methods. If the pattern is distribution free, then adopt nonparametric methods.

This you may decide on the observation of the pattern of distribution that you get from your pilot study or from other available sources. However, it may be noted that the parametric statistics is better for fine discrimination and accuracy.

If your research is on the cause-effect relationship between the independent variable and the dependent variable, by controlling all the extraneous variables, then your study is at the highest level of hierarchy i.e. at the descriptive +classificatory +correlative+ explanatory level. In such cases, you may have to use high level statistics for establishing a mathematical model for prediction of one variable from the other. If your research study is not at this level, but below at the 3rd or 2nd level, then it is unnecessary to use high level statistics to impress others or for its own sake. Statistics is only a tool for its use appropriate to your requirements. Statistics is for research and research is not for statistics unless the research is on statistics itself.

Applications of statistical methods and techniques in social sciences are for the following purposes:

1.   Selection of the target population and the sample of that population.

2.   Quantification and measurement of the variables

3.   Checking the pattern of distribution of data for adopting parametric or nonparametric statistical methods.

4.   Refining the quality of tools prepared for the collection of data by checking the reliability and validity of such instruments

5.   Checking the similarities and differences through correlations, t-test, ANOVA, MANOVA and many other statistical methods

6.   Checking the concomitant variations of two or more variables to establish the cause- effect relationships

7.   Establishing the statistical base for your conclusions and generalizations.

You have to be familiar with all the statistical methods that you have employed for data collection and data interpretation. Use of SPSS without understanding the statistical assumptions behind the data processing, may land you in trouble, if someone asks questions on the statistical methods used for analyses and interpretations. Your input of data in a machine and the output that you receive from that machine do not show your academic strength, unless you are familiar with the statistical methods adopted for purpose.

Two statistical issues are raised for your further thoughts on the sample size and tests of significance.

The sample size issue:

Three terms are often used in connection with the kind and number of respondents to a study: the **universe**, the **population** and the **sample.** The universe consists of all possible respondents on certain selected attributes/variables at the global level for arriving at universal laws and principles as in physical sciences. The term 'infinite population' may be used under the concept 'universe'. The 'finite population' is only a sub unit of the universe – people confined to a particular category of your study or all the people of your target group. The 'sample' consists of the representative units of the target population. Pre-school children of Kerala, or pre-school children of Ernakulam district or pre-school children of Kalamassery municipality makes a lot of difference in the targeted population and the sample selected for the purpose. Your conclusions and generalizations are to be restricted to the target population, if your research is a descriptive survey type. But if your research is a process type with focus on the cause effect relationship between two variables, the conclusions and generalizations have validity beyond the region of your research. Firstly, decide on the kind of research you have taken up. The content oriented research with data on the present state of affairs is primarily for better planning and for taking certain policy decisions by the authorities on some issues pertaining to economic, social and political matters. Conclusions and generalizations have their own limitations based on the local and regional samples and the size of the sample whereas researches for understanding the connections between two variables have no such restrictions of the regions for generalizations. One is a content oriented and the other is a process oriented. The descriptive survey type research is content oriented and the hypothesis testing cause-effect related research is process oriented. There is substantial difference between these two types of research in methodology including the sample size. If the data distribution is normal, even a small sample is sufficient for conclusions and generalizations in the case of process type research. If data distribution is not normal bell shaped even a large number is not sufficient for the use of parametric methods. A large number of the sample is taken on the assumption that the distribution is likely to be normal based on the Central Limit Theorem. Increase in the sample size is always desirable as the accuracy will always improve with large size sample. But under certain conditions it may not be possible and hence the suggestion that even with small size sample, if the distribution adheres to an approximate normal distribution that is sufficient. The only requirement is that the sample size, if below certain level may likely to result in the acceptance of the null hypothesis whereas in reality it may not be so. Consider this aspect in relations to the type I and type II errors when you accept or reject the null hypothesis.

The Table given under appendix V shows the minimum sample you have to take as per the target population. You may take 10% more than the minimum to overcome the problems of non-responses and defective responses. But, if you get a normal distribution of data even with far less than the minimum given in the table that is sufficient for you to go ahead with your research activities. It is the logic that matters, not the size of the sample per se. Two conditions for the selection of the sample and the sample size are: (1) unbiased sample to represent the target population and (2) Normal distribution of data, especially data pertaining to the dependent variable with the spread of standard deviations beyond 1.96 on either side of the mean. If these two conditions are not fulfilled, the probability of confirming the null hypothesis is high. Normal distribution is not an absolute requirement if you are ready to adopt statistical methods of the nonparametric statistics.

A question that may arise in your mind at this stage is the normality of data distribution of the variables. Does it cover all the variables under the study? Or is it confined to the independent or dependent variable or both? It may not be possible to cover all variables. Sometimes, the independent variable may be discrete categories such as gender, regions or different stages by age. But, such categorical variables are not desirable in the case of dependent variable, the phenomenon under observations. So, the normal distribution of data is more relevant to the dependent variable and not on other variables of the study.

Test of Significance issue:

"What is so significant about significance"? This question was raised by many investigators on the tradition of putting 0.05 and 0.01 levels of significance for a generalization from the sample to the population. The answer is that it is only a tradition accepted by the scientific community and there are no further explanations. If it is 0.01 and less the conclusions and generalizations is very strong and if it is in between 0.05 and less up to 0.01 of significance, it is acceptable. If it is >0.05 and <0.10, by the same logic we may say that there is a strong trend in rejecting the null hypothesis. It is just a tradition and nothing else.

By an index of significance, we need not come to the conclusion that the cause effect relationship is well established. The term 'significance' only implies that the observation is consistent and accurate and the error will not exceed 5% or 1% and no further meaning is to be attached to the term. Significance level by itself is not sufficient, the strength should also be considered, as the level of significance is a function of the sample size. There are instances wherein the difference between two variables is small with high significance and no significance with large difference and this is due to the small or large sample size. Think of the situation where the correlation between two variables is 0.95, but it is insignificant due to a small size and another situation where the r=0.13, but highly significant with a large sample. It is the sample size that makes the difference in significance. The causal connection is to be arrived by your research design and methodology and not by the level of significance per se. The same pattern of data with a large size sample can make the findings significant. Therefore, you have to take sufficient caution in the interpretations and at deriving conclusions and arriving at generalizations.

CHAPTER XI
Summary of Steps in an
explanatory type empirical Research

1.   Start with a tentative subject area of your research interest and read available relevant literature. Discuss with your guide and other experts on the possibility of a meaningful research topic within the subject area. Narrow down your review of literature to the topic selected by you. Doing research on a topic given by your guide or any other expert may not create the required enthusiasm essential for your commitment to your research activities. Spend at least six months for the review of literature in your area of interest for the final decision on the selection of the topic for research.

2.   Clarify and specify the dependent variable (DV). This DV is the phenomenon under your observation. Prepare a long list of all possible variables that affect the DV and that variable that you assume is the most important one that influence DV be selected as the independent variable (IV) and all others as extraneous variables to be excluded, controlled or kept as moderating, mediating and intervening variables in your study. Literature review will help you to identify and specify the variables.

3.   Conceptual clarity of every variable by apt definitions is essential. Existing theories on the phenomenon under observations are also necessary to provide a theoretical framework for your study.

4.   Discuss the relevance of the variables in your study with your guide and others who are in a position to help you for further clarifications. If a particular variable is more qualitative than

quantitative, explore the possibility of their quantification for measurement by an operational definition of the concept/variable. If it is difficult to quantify and if they are not the DV and IV, keep such variables as categorical attributes/variables.

5.   Decide on the independent variable that could be the cause of the dependent variable. An independent variable is always antecedent to the dependent variable. The cause always precedes the effect. Other variables are either associated with the IV or DV and as such the sequence may be antecedent, concurrent or consequent with the IV and DV. Take care that the consequences of DV is not a part of the research design; it is only a supplementary study to the main study as the effect of the original DV become the DV of the original DV which is now transformed as an IV of the supplementary study.

6.   Prepare a tentative research design showing the temporal sequence of all variables and the inter connectedness of these variables with the hypotheses that you formulate on the basis of literature survey. Before deciding the research design, you must have a clear picture on the associations of all these variables by correlations and factor analysis to be aware of the homogeneity within and between the various variables.

7.   If it is already available from available literature, the design is OK. But if you do not have such information in advance, you may have to collect data from a pilot study and based on such data you have to refine the research design made earlier. A research design is a blue print for further research activities.

8.   Prepare the tools/instruments for data collection before the pilot study. Get it approved by the guide. For each variable in your study appropriate tools are required. Also take care of the discomfort and inconvenience of the respondents in giving their responses to the tools and instruments that you are going to use. A very lengthy response sheets may be resented by the respondents. Make it as short as possible. The instruments for measurement of certain variables also may need refinement in terms of easy comprehension on the part of the respondents and also for assessing the reliability and validity of the instrument

from the data supplied by the respondents. This is possible only by a pilot study.

9.   Decide the target population and the area of study. Prepare the sample frame and follow the sampling method to avoid bias in selecting the sample. From the required sample size, select another small sample for the pilot study.

10.   Data from the pilot study are to be used for the refinement of the research design and also the tool/instrument for data collection from a larger sample.

11.   If everything is ok up to this stage, do the field work of data collection from the entire sample. If necessary, the data collected from the pilot study can also be considered, if no modification was included in the instrument for data collection. If there are modifications in the instrument, you may have to approach them once again.

12.   Once you collect all the required data, process it with the help of SPSS or other statistical packages, with full understanding of the statistical methods appropriate to your requirements. Data presentations, interpretations and discussions of your conclusions and generalization are the main part of your study and if you go wrong in this section, everything goes wrong in your research work. This part is your own original work. Your thesis is judged on the basis of this section, in addition to your scholarship by way of review of literature and references made. Literature review is a continuous process throughout your research, especially for quoting the study findings of other researchers with your findings.

13.   Resort to statistical analyses, if data are primarily for serving the following purposes: (1) to find out the degree of similarities among the variables (the method of agreement) (2) to find out the degree of differences (the method of differences) (3) to find out both the methods of agreement and differences (Joint method of agreement and difference) and (4) to establish the relationship between DV and IV for prediction of one from the other (the method of concomittant variations). These causative principles are essential for an explanatory type of research even in social sciences.

14.   Prepare the first draft of your thesis and get it approved by your guide. The thesis should include the following:
Introductory; Review of literature; Scope and methodology with focus on the research design; data presentation, data analyses, data interpretation in the form of conclusions/generalizations; summary of conclusions and generalizations, including theoretical implications and practical applications of your findings, scope for further research and possible limitations of your study. The text is immediately followed by a list of references. Some more details not given in the text are given in the appendices to the text.

15.   Polish your thesis by a second draft in consultation with an expert in English language to check spelling and grammar mistakes and the style of presentation. The physical appearance of the bounded volume is to be attractive. Adhere to all the conditions stipulated by the University for the acceptance of your thesis.

16.   You need not bother much about the evaluation of your thesis, if you have taken enough care at every stage of your research. Your actions will justify the reward.

This book is only a guide book for research scholars to help them to get away with their confusions and worry. For details on certain points, you may have to consult some text books on Research methods and methodology and also books on statistics for better understanding of statistical methods. The logic of deriving conclusions and arriving at generalization is the main focus of this guide book. The purpose is served well, if you find this book useful to you.

<u>References:</u>

Allport, G.W. (1962)
"The General and the Unique in Psychological Science"
Journal of Personality, 30, 405-422.

Allport, G.W. (1937)
Personality: A Psychological Interpretation
New York: Henry Hold.

Bacon, Francis. (1620; 1878)
Novum Organum (New Instrument).
(First publication in Latin (1620) and subsequent
publication in English; Clarendon Press, 1878.)
(SS: www.brita.com/EB checked/topic/42129/
Novum- organum   ) . Date of reference: 07/02/2014

Guttman, L. (1950)
"The Basis for Scalogram Analysis" in Stouffer et.al. Measurement
and Prediction".
The American Soldier Vol. IV
New York: Wiley.

Likert, Rensis. (1932)
"A Technique for the Measurement of Attitudes"
Archives of Psychology, 140: 1-55.

Mill, James Stuart. (1843)
*A System of Logic, Ratiocinative and Inductive, Being a Connected
View of the Principles of Evidence, and Method of Investigation.* Vol.I.
London: John W Parker, West Strand.
(SS: en.wikipedia.org/wiki/Mill's_Methods)
Date of reference: 07/02/2014

Thorndike, E.L. (1926)
The Measurement of Intelligence.
New York: Teacher's College, Columbia University.

Thurstone, L.L. (1959)
The Measurement of Values.
Chicago: University of Chicago Press.

Glossary of Relevant Terms in Research Methodology and Statistics

Abductive reasoning: The intellectual process of deriving conclusions from conditional statements with the express 'if,... then ...". This is also often called the hypothetico-deductive logic.

Action Research: For better understanding of social relations problems and the group dynamics, certain social groups are created with the intention of observing the parameters/ variables that contribute to the success or failures of small social groups. Studies of small group research also belong to this category. Impact of social variables on social activities and functions are observed and analysed in such action research.

Alpha error: The hypothesis is accepted as true, when it could be false and the null hypothesis could be true (see Type I error).

Analytical Research: Research studies with quantitative measurements to get certain conclusions or at arriving certain generalization based on data analyses, as opposed to pure descriptive research. It is also called as quantitative research, opposite to qualitative.

ANOCOVA: Same as ANOVA, but adds control of one or more covariates that are likely to influence the dependent variable. When an independent variable tries to control the influence of some other uncontrolled variables, such an uncontrolled variable is sometimes called the covariate or the concomitant variable. Statistical method of data analysis in such cases is the analysis of covariates.

ANOVA: Analysis of variance is a statistical method to test the significance of differences among more than two variables at a time.

ANOVA – One way: Analysis of variance with an independent variable with several sub variables constituting a single one factor and its association with the dependent variable

ANOVA – two way: Analysis of variance with two or more independent variables constituting more than one factor, and their associations with the dependent variable.

Antecedent conditions: Conditions that come before the occurrence of a variable; The Independent variable is always an antecedent variable to the dependent variable.

Antecedent variables: variable that comes before another variable in a temporal sequence

APA system: The reference system given by the American psychology Association.

Applied research: Research Studies to solve practical problems using the findings of research for a specific purpose i.e. Research with a definite purpose for solving an observed problem or application of the research findings for the benefits of mankind.

'A' proposition: A universal positive statement. E.g. 'All men are mortal'.

Area Sampling: When a list of population or the sample frame is missing or not available, and the study is in a large geographical area to be covered, one may resort to sub areas excluding overlapping and take a random samples from different small areas for the survey. This will help in collecting data simultaneously from different area settings.

Attribute: A characteristic, qualitative or quantitative, of an object, event, person or situation.

Beta error: Acceptance of the null hypothesis as true when it could be false and the alternative hypothesis could be true. (See Type II error)

Bibliography: A long list of books and articles on the subject of your research, including references made in the text.

Binary digits: A set of two digits, 0 and 1 for measurement as in the computer

Bipolar: Measurement on both directions ranging from extreme negative to an extreme positive with a neutral middle point.

Canonical correlations: An additional procedure to the usual calculation of correlation when you require simultaneous computation of multi variables both on the independent and dependent sides.

Canonical analysis: A statistical method of simultaneous prediction of a set of dependent variables from their joint covariance with a set of independent variables.

Case studies: Another version of the clinical type research (see clinical type research)

Categorical attributes: An attribute/characteristic without any quantitative variation; a classificatory object/event or situation.

Categorical variables: An attribute/characteristic based on categorization of quantitative variations

Causal analysis: Study of how variations in one variable result in variations on the other with a clear picture on the antecedent and consequent temporal sequence of cause- effect relations.

Causal variable: Another name for the independent variable

Causative principles of J.S.Mill: The five methods of arriving at the cause-effect relationships are: The method of Agreement; the method of Difference; the Joint methods of Agreement and Difference; The method of concomitant variation and the method of Residue.

Cause-effect relationship: Association of two variables wherein one is the causal antecedent and the other is the effect consequence.

Central Limit Theorem: A mathematical theorem stating that the sum of the observations (mean) taken from a population tends to become normal, when the number of observations becomes very large. Even if the population is not normal in its distribution, a large sample is likely to take the shape of a normal distribution as per the Central limit theorem. The relationship between the shape of the population distribution and the shape of the sample distribution of the mean is known as the Central Limit Theorem.

Chi-square: Independent or dependent relationship between two or more sets of variables in nonparametric statistics. The actual observation of frequencies are compared with the theoretical expected frequencies in different categories to work out the chi-square values and interpreted with reference to a table with due consideration for the degrees of freedom.

Chronback's Alpha: A measure or coefficient of internal consistency that establishes reliability of a test/ an instrument.

Classificatory Research: Categorization of objects, events etc based on similarities and differences that one observes in Nature. The science of botany is the best example for the classificatory research.

Clinical Research: The focus of research is on a particular individual with a purpose of understanding him or his personal problems of adjustment or his physical /mental illness. Certain conclusions are derived from diagnosis, but no generalization is possible, unless a large number of similar cases are taken for a detailed study. The approach is more ideographic than nomothetic.

Cluster analysis: Method of classifying variables into clusters; a cluster consists of variables that correlate highly with one another and have comparatively low correlations with variables in other clusters.

Cluster sampling: Grouping of population into certain segments and samples are taken from such groupings or clusters. Grouping of population in some cases can be in the form of stratifications.

Completely random design (C.R. Design): An investigation design in which both replication and randomization are introduced at the same time.

Composite standard method: A method advocated by J.P. Guilford for developing an interval scale from the paired comparison ordinal data.

Conceptual: Relating to abstract ideas or a common term that indicates the unity among diversities.

Conclusions/Inferences: information drawn by data analyses.

Concomitant variations: An empirical relationship wherein the magnitude of one variable changes with the magnitude of the other variable (See co-variation)

Concurrent validity: Agreement between two standardized tests; of your own and the other a well accepted test for comparison with your test. If the agreement is high, then it is assumed that your test is valid as the other test is accepted as a valid one.

Concurrent variables: variable that comes simultaneously with another variable in a temporal sequence

Conditional logic: (see Abductive logic)

Confidence level: The p-value of 0.05 or 0.01 level or 95% or 99% of confidence on the consistency and accuracy of data or inferences from the data for a particular purpose.

Confounding relations: When the dependent variable is not completely free from the influence of an extraneous variable, the relationship between the independent and dependent variable is said to be a confounded relationship.

Confounding variables: Extraneous variables that are statistically correlated with the independent / dependent variable.

Connotation of a term: The meaning conveyed by the subject or the predicate of a proposition

Consequent variables: Variables that come after the independent/dependent variables in a temporal sequence. Moderating variable on IV after the occurrence of IV is a consequent moderating variable which functions as a mediating moderation. Consequent variables to DV are not taken in a research design as it is a DV to the original DV and the original DV becomes the antecedent IV. However, a study on the effect of the original DV can be a supplementary study to the original study with its own other variables.

Construct: An assumed existence of something that does not have a physical existence. If the abstract idea is based on commonality of diverse objects and events, then it is a concept; if it is only an abstraction on an assumed existence of something that does not exist physically, then it is a construct. Brain does exist, but intelligence is only a constructs it does not exist physically though intelligence is associated with brain.

Construct validity: A test/instrument is structured on a theoretical or conceptual attribute to be measured and a recheck on the test score with the theoretical proposition indicates the construct validity of the instrument.

Content Analysis: The recorded verbal materials in a schedule used along with the interview are subjected to detailed analysis either in a descriptive way or in quantitative form. In a questionnaire the responses are structured and hence it is subjected to quantitative analysis, but such quantification is not possible in a depth interview. Preparation of a questionnaire on the basis of schedule with an interview is, however, possible.

Content oriented research: When the purpose of the research is on the facts and figures for planning and problem solving rather than establishing associations and differences among the variables.

Content validity: A recheck whether the item statements in an instrument really reflect the concept/construct for the measurement of the attribute by seeking the opinions of experts on the subject.

Continuous series: A set of numbers varying in degree in an ascending or descending order i.e. a condition of more or less.

Contradictory statements: A universal positive statement and a particular negative statement are contradictory for acceptance of one denies the existence of the other; so is the case between a universal negative and a positive particular statement. If all men are mortal, it is a contradiction to make a statement that some men are not mortal. If no men are mortal, then, some men are mortal is a contradiction.

Contrary statements: No men are mortal is a contrary statement to all men are mortal or vice-versa. If one statement is accepted as true, then one cannot accept the other as true. But, if one is not true, the other may or may not be true.

Convenient sampling: (see deliberate sampling)

Copula: the verb in the predicate that links the subject and predicate.

Correlation: Association between two variables or among several variables ranging from +1.00 to -1.00. The minus correlation indicates association in the reverse i.e. high score in one variable and low score in the other.

Correlation analysis: Study of joint variation of two or more variables for determining the amount of association between such variables

Correlative research: Studies with major focus on associations among the variables and the number of factors that emerge out by a factor analysis.

Covariance: Variations in one variable result in a corresponding variation in the other as an indication of their relationships. It is another expression for concomitant variation.

Criterion related validity: A broad term that includes predictive validity and concurrent validity. Predictive validity indicates the usefulness of a test in making prediction on future performance and concurrent validity refers to similar findings of a test in other tests of the same attribute already known and well established.

Cross sectional Vs Longitudinal research: Research at a point of time is cross sectional and research on time series or at different times to see the impact of the changes in time is longitudinal. A study on child development is longitudinal. Comparison of a particular stage of development among children of different cultures is cross sectional.

Cross tabulation: Classification of each variable into two or more categories and then cross classify the variables into subcategories. Interactions among the categories and subcategories could be symmetrical, asymmetrical or reciprocal. It starts with a two way table which indicates whether there is or there is not an interrelationship and among the variables.

Cumulative Scale: Guttmann's scale wherein only a few statements are given with pre set values arranged in an ascending order of values. Acceptance one statement implies the acceptance of all statements below and the value of the statement in the hierarchy of statements is accepted as the data.

Data analysis: Application of statistical methods for arriving at descriptive statistics as well as inferential statistics in order to derive conclusions and arrive at generalizations.

Data collection: Getting the responses from individuals of the sample through a questionnaire or field work with an interview schedule.

Data inferences: The intellectual process of deriving conclusions from general propositions or premises.

Data interpretation: Meaning of the findings of data analyses in the framework of your research objectives/problems/ hypotheses.

Deductive Process: A system of deriving inferences and conclusions from propositions /premises /data by the science of reasoning or logic.

Deliberate sampling: A non probability sampling with a definite purpose i.e. deliberate selection of sample items which is likely to suffer from personal bias and prejudices; whether such samples are true representatives of the population is doubtful. If such samples are as per the convenience of the researcher, then it is called convenience sampling. Judgmental sampling is another form of the same procedure. Such samples may be used in descriptive research and also for hypotheses formation for more rigorous scientific research.

Denotation: The quantitative extent of the subject or predicate often expressed as 'all', 'some', 'none', 'some not', etc.

Dependent Variable: The phenomenon under investigation, the central focus of the study (the Y in $Y=f(X)$ expressions).

Descriptive Vs analytical research: (see qualitative Vs quantitative)

Descriptive research: Narrative report with focus on facts and figures without any attempt at data analyses for finding out similarities, differences, correlations, cause-effective relations of variables.

Descriptive statistics: simple presentation of data summary in the form of the central tendency, dispersion of data, percentage associations, differences etc without its relationship to the population parameters. It is a univariate description of the state of affairs in the form of data summary.

Diagnostic research: (see clinical type research)

Differences: Heterogeneity among the variables opposed to similarity. If the mean and standard deviation of a particular attribute are significantly different in two groups, we may assume that the groups are taken from two different populations.

Differential Scale: Another name for the Thurstone's type equal appearing interval scale by using judges to differentiate the degree of differences among the statements on a continuum ranging from extreme negative attitude values to extreme positive attitude values.

Difficulty level: What per cent of the respondents is giving the correct answer to a question asked? The item could be 'very easy', 'easy', 'neither easy nor difficult', 'difficult' or 'very difficult'. Answers to such questions are in terms of the difficulty level or percent of respondents giving the answers. If the correct answer is given 100% respondents, it is very easy and if only 10% is giving the correct answer, the item is difficult.

Discrete numbers: Categorical numbers without continuity.

Discrete variables: Categorical attributes or categorical variables derived from classifications of continuous series of numbers.

Discrimination index: When we divide the total respondents into an upper level group (top 25%) and lower level group (bottom 25%) based on the total scores obtained from the respondents, these two groups will enable us to find out the discrimination values of each item in the test. If the high group response to an item is 'correct ' or 'true', then the Low group response to the same item should be 'wrong' or 'False' in order to differentiate or discriminate the item. If it is the same percent for both the criterion groups the item does not discriminate the two known groups. Discrimination index is based on such logic i.e. differentiating two known groups in their performance on the same item.

Distributed denotation: If the subject of a proposition denotes a complete set (all or none), it is assumed to be distributed to include each and every items of the subject. It is either universal positive or a universal negative proposition. In the universal negative proposition, even the predicative term is distributed. In particular negative proposition, only the predicative term is distributed.

Distribution free statistics: Another name for nonparametric statistics

Distribution of data: When an obtained data are plotted on a graph with the frequencies of their occurrences on the 'y' axis, the pattern of distribution may take different shape such as the bell shaped normal distribution, skewed to the left or right, leptokurtic or mesokurtic. If it is a distribution that involves parameters, it is parametric, otherwise it is nonparametric or distribution free statistics.

Effect variables: (same as the dependent variable)

Empirical: Based on testing of experience or observations based on experience as opposed to conceptual or theoretical without actual data as evidence or proof.

Empirical Research: Research based on direct experience of the respondents (observations of the researchers or data) for detailed analyses for deriving conclusions and arriving at generalizations.

'E' Proposition: A universal negative statement. E.g. 'No men are mortal'

Equivalent Form method: A method to test the reliability of a test by requesting the same individual to respond to two sets of the test, both of them measuring the same attribute, but given in two different forms.

Experimental Vs control groups: When two groups of equivalent nature are selected for a study with the difference that one group is treated with the presence of the independent variable and the other group is treated without the presence of the independent variable and later they are compared with reference to a particular attribute or performance, the difference is accounted by the presence of the independent variable. The group treated with the presence of the independent variable is known as the experimental group and the group without the presence of the independent variable is known as the control group.

Experimental design: Observations under controlled conditions; Study of the impact of the independent variable on the dependent variable by excluding all extraneous variables that may affect the IV or DV.

Experimental Research: Observations under controlled conditions wherein the effect of all extraneous variables are nullified by appropriate methods, especially by certain instruments. This is the classical method with one independent and one dependent variable at a time.

Explanatory research: Research with focus on the cause-effect hypotheses testing type studies.

Exploratory Research: Studies in a relatively unexplored area wherein research publications are found rare and the researcher is a pioneer in the field.

Ex post facto research: A descriptive study just reporting the state of affairs as they are without any control of the variables.

Extraneous variables: All variables other than the dependent and independent variables which affect the DV or IV and are to be controlled.

Evaluative research: A research study to evaluate the effectiveness of a project, system or method, after the implementations. The effectiveness of a particular training programmes or the effectiveness of pedagogy in teaching system is an evaluative research.

Factor Analysis: A multivariate technique of research when there is a systematic interdependence among a set of variables at the manifest level and the researcher is interested in identifying the fundamental or latent factors that create the commonality among the variables.

Factorial design: When there are many factors both in the independent and dependent variables, the research design is factorial. A simple factorial design consists of two factors and it is made complex by more than two factors at a time.

Fallacy of ambiguous middle term: If the middle term has different meanings in the two premises, it commits the fallacy of ambiguous middle.

Fallacy of illicit major: If the predicate of the conclusion is distributed, then that term in the premise should also be distributed. Violation of this requirement results in the fallacy of illicit major.

Fallacy of illicit minor: If the subject of the conclusion is distributed, then the same term in the premise should also be distributed. Violation of this requirement is the fallacy of the illicit minor.

Fallacy of two negative propositions: Denial of two premises does not lead to any conclusion.

Fallacy of two particular propositions: Two particular propositions do not lead to any conclusion.

Fallacy of undistributed middle term: If the middle terms in both the premises are undistributed, then it commits the fallacy of undistributed middle.

Field observations/Research: Research based on data collected from the field by different methods and approaches. Observations made by the researcher by going into the field for data collections.

Finite population: A population where the items can be counted to a definite level, even if the population size is very large.

Fundamental research: Research studies on a phenomenon for its own sake with the purpose to enhance the frontiers of knowledge without any concern for its use in solving practical problems; A research for its own sake to understand the nature of a phenomenon without any concern for problem solving or applications for its practical uses.

Generalizations: extension of the inferences and conclusions from the sample to the population by checking the homogeneity of data distributions of different variables.

Guttmann's cumulative type scale: (see cumulative scale)

Harvard system of giving references: The reference system given by the Harvard University

Historical research: Research on the past to the present of an object, person, event, or a situation in a chronological order or subject wise with interpretations or reinterpretations; Historical research can be in any field of enquiry. Generally, it is more descriptive and qualitative than quantitative and analytical.

H-test: (see Kruskal-wallis H-test)

Hypothesis (H1):   A statement with assumption that x is the cause of y or x is associated with y in certain direction. All statements are not hypothesis; only if the statement makes an assumption on a possible relationship between the dependent and independent variables, it becomes a hypothesis.

Hypothesis testing research: Research for accepting or rejecting the hypothesis or assumption that the independent and dependent variables are related.

Hypothetico-deductive logic: (See Abductive logic)

Ideographic: What is applicable to one based on his/her uniqueness. Generality of the findings is doubtful; it is unique to one rather than general to all/most.

Immediate inference: An inference from a single proposition.

Independent variable: That variable which is assumed to be the antecedent one to the dependent variable and assumed to be the cause of the dependent variable (the X in $Y=f(X)$ expression)

Inductive logic: The intellectual process of arriving at a general statement from observation of several specific cases; the process from specifics to general.

Inductive process: a system of arriving at generalization from sample to population or from specific instances to general statements; the intellectual process of arriving at a general statement from observation of several specific cases.

Inferences: Synonymous with conclusion from one or more propositions.

Inferential statistics: A branch of statistics that helps us to draw inferences, conclusions and generalizations on a phenomenon from available data and also to check whether such inferences and conclusions of the sample are equally applicable to the population of the sample. Inferential statistics are used for estimations and extension of such inferences/conclusions to the population.

Infinite population: When there is no limitation to the number of items in a set of population, one may call it an infinite population.

'I' Proposition: A particular positive statement. E.g. 'Some men are mortal'.

Instruments: Standardized tests or physical instruments for several purposes. The functions of mechanical instruments in a laboratory research are: introducing the independent variable and recording it; recording the dependent variable; controlling the extraneous variables etc. In field research in social sciences the instruments are confined to the schedule, questionnaire and tests and in some exceptional cases some electronic instruments depending on the nature of the research.

Interaction effect: The joint effect of two variables on another variable. Variable A by itself may not have any effect on D; Variable B by itself may not have any effect on D. But A and B together may have some effect on D. The combined effect of two variables on another variable is called the interaction effect of A and B on D.

Interactive variations: In ANOVA treatment of data, the residual effect of the relationship between the left-over sums of squares and the left-over degrees of freedom is known as the interaction variation.

Inter-quartile range: A measure of statistical dispersion of the mid-range or the middle fifty i.e. Q3-Q1. You get inter-quartile deviation by dividing Q3-Q1 by 2. It is also known as quartile deviation.

Interval Scale: Keeping the distance between two adjacent numbers in a series equal throughout the scale with an arbitrary starting point.

Intervening variables: Interactive effect of mediating variables on DV

Interview: Personal contact with the respondents for seeking information/responses and recording them for further analysis.

Item analysis: Statistical methods of finding out the difficulty level and discrimination value of each item for discarding items which are found to be irrelevant or duplications, in a set of questions or statements in a test.

Joint method of agreement and difference: When x is present, y is also present and when y is absent x is also absent. The combination of the method of agreement and the method of difference ensures the cause-effect relationship.

Judgemental sampling: (see deliberate sampling)

Kendal's coefficient of correlation: A nonparametric measure of relationship among three or more sets of variables. If there are only two sets of variables and the N is small, the method usually adopted is the Spearman's rank order correlation.

Kruskal-wallis H-test: A nonparametric test for inference that the sample distribution represents the population distribution. It is similar to the one way analysis of variance without the assumption of normal distribution of the population or a population having the same standard deviation.

Kurtosis: More or less frequency of occurrence of values at the centre in comparison with the normal curve. If more, it is mesokurtic (peak) and if less it is leptokurtic (flat)

Laboratory based experimental research: Experiments conducted in a laboratory setting.

Latent structure analysis: Factor analysis method starts with a correlation matrix of all variables. If a particular variable is non metric (categorical attribute) you cannot proceed with correlation of this variable with other metric variables. In such cases you cannot ignore the presence of categorical attribute too. The effect of such latent factors not manifested through quantitative measurements is to be inferred by logical interpretations.

Latin Square Design: When there are many variables and degree variations within each variable, to establish cause-effect relationship becomes difficult, especially to study all the variables at the same time. The model of experimental design adopted in agriculture in the form of various plots or blocks with differential treatments of each block/plot is an example. Different soil fertility, different types of seed, different fertilizers, different methods of irrigation etc are to be considered when the health and growth of a pant is the dependent variable. The study cannot be done simultaneously, but is feasible when there are different plots to conduct research by differential treatment of the plots. Latin square design or L.S design may help in such situations.

Law of comparative judgement: For conversion of the ordinal scale by paired comparison method to an interval scale, the law of comparative judgement method was developed by Thurstone. The technique is conversion of frequencies of preferences given by the judges into a table of proportions which are then transformed into Z matrix. J.P Guilford refined it further by his Composite Standard method.

Leptokurtic: When the distribution of data shows high peak and flat tails meaning that most of the data are clustered around the mean, it is leptokurtic.

Library research: Research by the use of published materials including the use of published secondary data without collecting primary data by one's own efforts.

Likert's summated type Scale: (see summated scale)

Logic: The science of reasoning with main thrust on deductive form for deriving conclusions and inductive form for arriving at generalizations to check the validity of conclusions and truthfulness of an expressed statement/proposition/premise.

Longitudinal research: (see cross sectional Vs Longitudinal research)

Major Premise: That premise in syllogism that contains the predicate of the conclusion.

MANOCOVA: Same as MANOVA but adds control of one or more covariates that may influence the DV

MANOVA: Same as ANOVA, but study two or more related DVs while controlling the correlations between the associated DVs

Mann-Whitney U-test: (see U-test)

Maximum likelihood: A statistical approach in which one maximizes some relationship between the sample of data and the population from which the sample are drawn.

Mean: The average of all values in a data set or distribution.
Median: Value that occupies the middle of a set of values when they are arranged in an ascending or descending order of the magnitude. The median divides the distribution into two equal parts.

Mediating variables: that variable which is in between the IV and DV which are classified as (a) mediating moderation on IV, (b) mediating moderation on DV and (c) interaction between mediating moderation on IV and mediating moderation on DV.

Measures of Associations: A measure to assert the similarities among several sets of variables showing either going together (positive) or in reverse (negative) directions.

Measures of Central Tendencies: The central value in a given distribution of scores obtained.

Measures of differences: Identifications of differences among different sets of variables and whether such differences are real or significant.

Measures of dispersions: Variations of scores in a given distribution

Measurement of relationships: Different correlations techniques to establish the associations between two variables or among several variables and also the cause effect relations between or among such variables by regression analysis techniques including multiple regression analysis. Establishing association by itself is not sufficient to establish the cause-effect relations; the antecedent-consequence temporal sequence is also very important.

Mesokurtic: When the distribution of data is widely spread with a lower height, it is called mesokurtic.

Method of Agreement: When the presence of x always results in the presence of y, it is a condition of agreement, but y may also be present in the absence of x indicating that y may be caused by factors other than x.

Method of concomitant variations: Changes in the degree of one variable resulting in changes in the other variable in a predictable manner indicates the possibility of a cause effect relationship between the two variables.

Method of Difference: Even in the absence of y there is the presence of x indicating that x could be present due to some other antecedent or concurrent conditions.

Method of Residue: In the presence of ABC we find the presence of def and we know that B and C are the causes of e and f. What is left out is A and d and so we come to the conclusion that A is the cause of d. This kind of inference is the method of residue, provided other variables are completely excluded from our observations

Methodology: Systems procedures and methods adopted in the research process from the beginning to the end.

Methods: Specific procedures and techniques for a particular purpose.

Middle Term: The common term in two premises that enable to us to draw a conclusion. No conclusion is possible unless at least one of them is distributed.

Minor Premise: In a syllogistic reasoning, that premise which contains subject of the conclusion is the minor premise.

Mode: The observation in a data set that exhibits the highest frequency or the most occurring value in a distribution.

Model: A mathematical formula for prediction of the level of y variable from x variable or vice-versa based on regression and other statistical analyses; formalization of relationship between variables in the form of mathematical equations; It is a mathematical formula to predict the relationship between the independent and dependent variables. From the obtained values of the independent variable, the value of the dependent variable is predicted and vice-versa too.

Moderating variables: Moderating variables are those variables among the extraneous variable that cannot be controlled, but whose effect on IV or DV is to be assessed by statistical methods.

Such variables that moderate the IV is called moderating variables on IV and that which moderates the DV is called the moderating variable on DV. Moderating variables could be antecedent or concurrent with the IV or DV, but not in between the IV and DV with arrow direction from IV $\rightarrow$ MV $\rightarrow$ DV

Multivariate analysis: Statistical method which analyses more than two variables simultaneously on a sample of observations. The concept includes multiple regression analysis, multiple discriminant analysis, multiple analysis of variance and canonical analysis.

Multi regression analysis: In multiple regression analysis, there are more than two variables at a time in the research design and their associations and causal connections are at the focus.

Multiple analyses of variance: Analysis of variance with multiple dependent and independent variables.

Multiple correlations: Simple correlation is the association of two variables at a time and the usual expression is 'r' for such simple correlation. If there are more than two variable at a time it is called multiple correlations and of the expression is 'R'. Square of 'R' is multiple coefficient of determination.

Multiple variables: When there are more than one independent variable and/or more than one dependent variables in a research design, it is a design with multiple variables.

Negative proposition: When the predicate denies the subject, then the proposition is negative.

Nominal Scale: Numbering a category as 1, 2, 3, etc to give an attribute a label.

Nomothetic: What is applicable to all rather than to one or some; general findings applicable to all members of a set.

Nonparametric statistics: If data obtained on an attribute/variable is not in tune with a parametric form of distribution, then it is nonparametric or distribution free statistics; statistical methods based on normal probability distribution should not be used in nonparametric or distribution free statistics. Other special methods are available for the treatment of the nonparametric statistics. Only nominal and ordinal scales are used in nonparametric statistics.

Normal distribution: A bell shaped curve showing perfect symmetry, based on the probability of occurrence with large sample.

Null hypothesis (H0): A statement with the assumption that there is no relationship between x and y variables, till it is rejected by the analyses of available data. Use of statistical methods is only for accepting or rejecting the null hypothesis. If null hypothesis (H0) is rejected, then indirectly you accept the hypothesis (H1) and if the null hypothesis is accepted, then indirectly you reject the hypothesis. It is because of this the hypothesis is often called as the alternative hypothesis to the null hypothesis.

Objective: The goals to be achieved within a time frame

Ordinal scale: Ordering the number as 1st, 2nd, 3rd, etc to show the relative order in a set of measurements.

Operational definition: Conversion of an abstract concept into an observable and tangible concept for quantification and measurement.

Operations Research: Also called a decision oriented research or a problem solving research wherein the focus is on systems analysis to find the right solution to a problem situation; the final outcome of such research is mathematical models for decision making.

'O' proposition: A particular negative statement. E.g. 'Some men are not mortal'.

Outliers: Deviant items (data) from the general pattern.

Parametric statistics: If data obtained on an attribute/variable shows a distribution depending on certain parameters based on the theory of probability, it is parametric wherein you are free to adopt interval and ratio scales of measurements.

Partial correlation: Partial correlation measures the degree of association between two random variables, with the effect of a set of controlling random variables removed.

Participative observation: If a research work is on the behaviour of people in a group in a socio- cultural setting, the researcher tries to become a participating member of such groups with close observations on the group process and other factors. Such a method is known as participatory observation method.

Particular negative proposition: A proposition is particular negative when the subject is undistributed and the predicate is distributed; the predicate denies the subject to make it negative.

Particular positive proposition: A proposition is particular positive when both the subject and predicate are undistributed and the predicate affirms the subject.

Particular proposition: A positive or negative proposition with an undistributed subject term.

Path analysis technique: A technique useful for decomposing the total correlation between any two variables in a casual system. It is based on a series of multiple regression analyses with the added assumption of causal connections between the dependent and independent variables.

Pearson coefficient correlation: A parametric statistical method for finding out the correlation between two variables.

Philosophy: The real meaning of philosophy is inquisitive ideational activities of the mind to understand the nature of all phinomena in this universe and from this general all inclusive concept later when there is maturity in each area of enquiry, such areas branched out as separate and independent fields of enquiry. Earlier every field of enquiry was a part of philosophy and so philosophy is called the mother of every academic subject. Today the field has been now reduced to a narrow area in the academic world, relating to spirituality, religion and other areas of enquiry. It is more an ideational arm chair speculations on the unknown to satisfy the curious minds.

Pilot study: A preliminary step in research to recheck data availability, data distribution, research design, reliability and validity of instruments for data collection and the problems experienced by the respondents in understanding the item in the questionnaire for a preliminary study with a sample of the sample. Actual data collection from the sample is to be done only after checking the responses of the respondents from this small sample.

Plagiarism: The unethical practice of not acknowledging the contribution of others; a sentence or a paragraph taken from the work of others, but writing it as if it is your own without

 any acknowledgment to the original author.

Population: A complete set of people appropriate to the attribute under study i.e. total number of people having the same attribute restricted to the targeted group.

Positive proposition: When the predicate is being attributed to the subject in a proposition, then the proposition is positive.

Predicate of the proposition: The predicate of a proposition is that of which something is said about the subject.

Prediction: Forecasting the future event in terms of probability.

Premises: Same as proposition when there are two with a middle term as in the case of a syllogism.

Probability theory: A mathematical theory on the prediction of occurrence of an event by understanding the pattern of outcomes in an experiment that can be repeated under the same conditions.

Problem: Perceived gap between the desired and the actual with a purpose to reduce it by research findings. It is also called as the problem solving research. Operations research is often problem solving research.

Problem oriented research: A research with focus on identification of problems and the ways and means of resolving such observed problem(s)

Process oriented research: When the purpose of a research is establishing associations, differences and co-variations among various variables in the study, it is a process oriented research.

Proposition: A categorical statement with a subject and a predicate; copula or the linking verb of the proposition is a part of the predicate.

Qualitative: An attribute which is not amenable to quantification and measurement

Qualitative Vs quantitative research: Research without any quantification of variables is descriptive and qualitative whereas research with quantified variables is quantitative and analytical

Quartile Deviation: Q3-Q1/2 i.e upper quartile (Q3) minus lower quartile (Q1) divided by two.

Quantification: The process of assigning numbers to an attribute for measurements.

Quantitative: An attribute which is amenable to quantification and measurements; measurement of an attribute in numbers

Questionnaire: A self reporting instrument with structured responses for collecting data from the respondents of the sample. The researcher need not personally contact the respondents, for everything is written in the instrument. Mail or e-mail system can be adopted for the distribution and collection of filled in questionnaire.

Quota sampling: A nonparametric sampling technique wherein a proportional quota of sample items from a stratified group is allocated, but within the quota allocated it is for the researcher to judge the actual sample to be included; in other words it is a combination of stratification, proportion of the sample to the population and judgemental sampling methods.

Random sampling method: selection of an item from the target population by lottery system on the assumption that there is high probability of sample distribution being similar to the population.

Use of random numbers is also often resorted to in such selection of items in the sample.

Range: The difference between the maximum and minimum scores in a given distribution.

Ratio scale: An interval scale with an absolute zero as the starting point.

References: Ideas, concepts, findings, opinions and explanations of other investigators that you have referred in your text of the thesis.

Regression analysis: Determination of the statistical relationship between two variables with an intention to establish the cause-effect relationship between the IV and DV; a statistical method to deal with the formulation of mathematical model depicting the relationship among variables which is used for the prediction of values of the dependent variable from the values of the independent variable.

Reliability: Self consistency within an instrument of measurement in the form of homogeneity of data; consistency of the responses given by the same person under the same conditions. Cronback's Alpha, test-retest method, Equivalent form method, split- half method etc are to find out the reliability of an instrument.

Research Design is a blue print for research activities with focus on all relevant variables and their interconnectedness in a temporal sequence and a pictorial presentation of the same.

Research ethics: The code of conduct to be followed by a researcher.

Research process: Research activities from its conception to its completion.

Sample: A portion of the target population that is unbiased to represent the whole population; a subset of the population. If it is the complete set of population it is called the census.

Sample frame: A comprehensive list of all items or units of the population available or prepared for selecting the sample on a random basis or by other sampling methods. e.g. telephone directory or a list available from the local panchayath on the house-holds in the area.

Sample size: What should be the number of items in a sample in accordance with the total items in the target population? This is decided on the basis of some statistical formula to ensure that the width of data distribution has to exceed the z-value of +/- 1.96 to avoid the probability of accepting the null hypothesis whereas in reality large sample size is likely to reject the null hypothesis. Sample size is the number of items in the sample in relations to the number of items in the target population. If it is considerably less, we may call it a small sample and if it is more than what is required, it is an unwanted large sample. A statistical formula is available on the required sample size to the population. The sample size far below the minimum required (small sample) and the sample size large beyond the requirements may create problems in the research outcome. The confidence level or probability that the observed value is within the precision limits of 95% or 99% that ensures that the probability of going wrong is only 5% or 1%. It is significant at p-value of 0.01 implies that the observation made may go wrong in the population only by 1% i.e. one can be sure of the consistency and accuracy of the findings.

Sample design: A definite plan before data collection based on the nature of population (target population of the study) and means and methods to ensure that no bias or prejudice have influenced the selection of sample items; the sample is to be a true representation of the target population. Planning in advance to select the nature and number of items in the population is to be done for the selection of sample items.

Sampling Design: A definite plan for obtaining sample from a given population and the procedure adopted for selecting the sample items.

Sampling error: Random variations in the sample estimates around the true population parameters in either direction and as such the expected value of such errors happens to be equal to zero. Sampling errors are likely to decrease with increase in the sample size.

Sampling methods: Methods of selecting a sample from the sampling frame for excluding possible bias. The selected sample is to be unbiased by avoiding any other considerations.

Sampling units: The sampling unit may take in the form of a region/location, a household, an institution or individual and such units are to be specified before deciding the sample.

Scale construction methods/ Scaling: Procedures of assigning numbers to attributes, especially to abstract concepts and constructs for a meaningful measurement. This is more so in the case of measuring attitudes and values. (See different scales of measurements, such as nominal, ordinal, interval and ratio)

Scales of measurements: different methods of measurement based on the nature in terms of existence (nominal scale), existence by a condition of more or less in quantity (ordinal scale), equal distance in between all the adjacent quantities (interval scale) and in definite proportions (ratio scale).   Methods of quantifications of varying degrees of precision for the measurement of opinions, attitudes and values, are often used in social science research.

Scalogram: The method of cumulative scale developed by Guttmann.

Schedule: Use of a schedule is required when the researcher is personally contacting the respondents for the collection of data; the schedule is only an outline of the area of enquiry with more freedom for the researcher to ask in-depth questions or structured responses to the given questions. Recording of the responses is to be done by the researcher with more freedom for the respondents to express his personal views. Interview with a schedule has its own advantages and disadvantage. Advantage is the freedom for both the researcher and the respondents and the major disadvantage is lack of a structure for proper quantitative analyses. If the information (responses) received from the respondents can be structured for quantifications, the disadvantages will fade away. Content analysis technique can be used for such purposes.

Scholarship Part of a research: Review of literature and references in the text that indicate the width and depth of background knowledge of the researcher.

Sequential sampling: Enlargement of sample units at different stages of the investigation, depending on the need. Sample of a sample of a sample is possible as the research progresses. The pilot study is to be done on a sample of a sample, rather than on an unrelated sample of the population.

Sign test: A nonparametric method of analysis based on the sign/ positive or negative directions indicated by the data.

Significance levels: Self consistency and accuracy of observational data at a particular level of probability. The confidence level or probability that the observed value is within the precision limits of 95% or 99% that ensures that the probability of going wrong is only 5% or 1%. It is significant at p-value of 0.01 implies that the observation made may go wrong in the population only by 1% i.e. one can be sure of the consistency and accuracy of the findings.

Similarities: Common features or associations among different variables necessary to find out the unity among diversities. There is homogeneity among different variable. If the mean and standard deviations of two groups are almost the same, we need not treat the two groups as separate as the score distribution is homogeneous. There are more similarities than differences between the two groups.

Skewness: More frequency of occurrence of data either to the right or left of the central value in a distribution of obtained data

Social sciences: A group of academic disciplines which have relevance in understanding social phenomena and social problems, such as economics, management, commerce, psychology, sociology anthropology, political science etc. There are sub-sets within social sciences, such as behavioural sciences consisting of psychology, sociology and anthropology.

Sources of errors: Possibilities of measurement errors are many due to the respondents, situations, instruments and by the nature of measurement itself. Each sources of measurement are to be checked for improving the quality of measurement.

Spearman's Rank order correlation: A nonparametric method of working out correlation between two variables

Split-half method of reliability: When a single test is divided into two parts, say all the odd items as one set and all the even items as another set and then working out the correlation between these two sets is the essence of the split-half method of reliability.

Standard deviation: deviation from the mean on either side in a probability distribution.

Standard error: The standard deviation of sampling distribution of a statistic is known as its standard error (S.E). It is considered to be a matter of chance. But if the difference happens to be more than 3 times of the SE, then it is not a chance error; it is due to something else than mere chance.

Statement: A categorical declarative sentence with a subject and a predicate; different from the interrogative and exclamatory or commanding type expressions

Statistics: The science of numbers (numerical data) and their analyses for interpretations resulting in conclusions and generalizations for the advancement of knowledge. It is a part of the mathematical science, but not a branch of mathematics.

The term 'statistic' is used for a specific set of data whereas the term 'statistics' in plural form refers to the entire field of the numerical science. The term **Statistic** refers to a function of the sample observations, for example, the mean of a sample.

Structural Equation Modelling: A statistical technique for testing and estimating causal relations between/among different variables. SEM may be exploratory or confirmatory depending on the nature of the problem; it is for predicting the outcome of the magnitude of one variable from our knowledge of the magnitude of another variable associated with the other variable.

Subaltern statements: Subaltern statements are the universal positive and particular positive on one side and universal negative and particular negative on the other side. Acceptance of the universal positive as true results in the acceptance of particular positive, but the reverse in not true. Similarly, acceptance of universal negative results in the acceptance of the particular negative, but not the reverse. From 'all' you can come to 'some', but from 'some' you cannot come to 'all'.

Sub- contrary statements: It is the relationship between two particular statements of which one is positive and the other negative. Acceptance of one as true does not results in the denial of the other. If some men are mortal that implies that some mortals are men; but it does not imply that some men are not mortal or some mortals are not men.

Subject of the proposition: The subject of a proposition is that of which we say make a statement.

Sub- variables: Different measures of the same variable or variables which are associated with the independent and dependent variables; If a variable has no significant association with another variable, then it becomes completely a different variable and not a sub variable.

Stratified random sampling method: If there are sub sets or sub groups within the target population, and if every such sub-sets is to be represented in the sample, prepare separate lists for each sub groups and then select items from each list by random methods.

Summated Scale: A Likert's type rating scale with numerical values for Strongly agree/agree/neither agree nor disagree/disagree/strongly disagree etc. The values are summated as data for further analyses.

Survey type descriptive research: Research by collection of facts and figures from the field by the use of questionnaire/schedule. Often such studies are descriptive on facts and figures rather than correlative and explanatory. A survey research can also be correlative and explanatory, if it is quantitative and process oriented one.

Syllogistic reasoning: A conclusion from two premises by the presence of a common term of which one is to be distributed.

Systematic random sampling: A modification to the random sampling by taking the first item by lottery followed by an nth item from the sampling frame. If the first item is the 8th from the list, then every 10th item from 8th onwards i.e. 8th,18th, 28th,38th etc with freedom to take the adjacent item in cases of non availability of the specified item. Selecting an item from a list of the target population by a lottery system and then opting every nth item from the list as the sample of the population.

Target population: Total items from a set population as per the nature of attribute under investigation.

Technique: A set of procedural activities for the solution of a problem or performance of a task.

Test-Retest reliability method: Testing an individual twice with the same test under similar conditions with a time gap in order to check the consistency of his/her performance.

Theoretical Research: Studies based on concepts and ideas without collecting relevant data from the field as opposed to empirical research

Theory: A group of ideas to explain an observed phenomenon; Elaboration of explanatory concepts relating to a phenomenon; concepts and their inter-relationships for explaining a phenomenon.

Thurstone's scale: Scale construction by the method adopted by Thurstone wherein the distance between two adjacent statements is determined by a set of judges.

Tools: Questionnaire, schedule, tests and similar instruments including the required statistical methods as a tool for collection and analysis of data.

Truthfulness of a proposition: If a given statement is the product of inductive reasoning, with facts and figures supporting the statement, then the statement is accepted as true. All men are mortal is true, but all men are honest may not be acceptable as true by all.

t-test: A parametric statistical method for checking the significance of difference between two variables at a time or testing the same attributes in two different group to identify their homogeneity or heterogeneity of the score distribution, usually with small groups than large sample.

Type I error: Rejecting the null hypothesis, when it is in fact true. (See Alpha error)

Type II error: Accepting the null hypothesis as true when it is in fact false (see Beta error)

Uncertainty: A state of having limited knowledge where it is difficult to describe the event exactly or predict the future with confidence.

Undistributed terms: When the subject or the predicate refers only to some and not to all, then the term is undistributed as in the case of the predicate term of the universal positive and the subject and the predicate terms of the particular positive and the subject term of the particular negative proposition.

Unipolar: One sided measurement either in a positive direction or in a negative direction; low positive to high positive or low negative to high negative.

Universal negative Proposition: A proposition is universal negative when both the subject and predicate are distributed and the predicate denies the subject.

Universal positive proposition: A proposition is universal positive when the subject is distributed, but not the predicate and the predicate affirms the subject.

Universe: The target group of population of the study at the global level not restricted to a region or a country. In practice Population and universe are the same; if it is infinite population, the relevance of universe is more for finite population may be restricted by some other considerations. Application of the process type research is more universal whereas applications of descriptive survey type research without any hypotheses have its own limitations to be restricted to a specific population.

U-test: A nonparametric test of null hypothesis that the two populations are the same against the alternative hypothesis that they are different. This is also known as Mann-Whitney U-test or Wilcoxon rank-sum test (Wilcoxon-Mann-Whitney test).

Validity: Validity is a measure to check whether the concept used really measures what it intended to measure by a number of criteria. There are several validity measures such as Face validity, concurrent validity, construct validity, predictive validity etc.

Validity of a conclusion: A conclusion drawn from the given proposition or premises devoid of logical fallacies is a valid conclusion and if the conclusion violates the basic tenants of logic, then it is an invalid conclusion. E.g. 'All crows are black' and 'some blacks are flying beings'; any conclusion inferred from these two premises is likely to be invalid as it commits the fallacy of the undistributed middle. The given premises may be true or untrue; but the conclusion could be invalid even if the premises are true or valid if the premises are untrue. In logic validity and truthfulness are two different things. A true and valid conclusion is often called as a strong conclusion.

Values: Numerical magnitude or quantity; p-value is the probability value from the normal distribution table.

Variable: Quantitative variations of an attribute in an ascending or descending order; if an attribute is nominal, it is called categorical attribute. If based on quantity, but only a classification it is called categorical variable as it is nominal. Even a categorical attribute such as gender is often called a variable, though there is no quantitative variation within the attribute.

Variance: Squared value of the standard deviation; spread of data distribution from the minimum to the maximum.

Varimax rotation: One of the methods in factor analysis to maximize the variance of loadings within each factor.

Wilcoxon-Mann-Whitney test: A nonparametric test to determine whether two independent samples have been drawn from the same population. (see U-test and Mann-Whitney test).

Z-score: Raw score minus the Mean divided by the standard deviation is the z-score of the distribution.

Z-test: A statistical method for judging the significance of several statistical measures, particularly the mean. It is based on the normal probability distribution. Z is worked out by subtracting the mean from the actual score and then dividing it by the standard deviation. A z score above +/- 1.96 is supposed to be sufficient for checking the normal distribution at the 0.05 level of significance.

BOOKS FOR YOUR REFERENCE

Ackoff, Russel. L., (1962)
Scientific Method,
New York: John Wiley & Sons.

Ackoff, Rusel. L., (1961)
The Design of Social Research,
Chicago: University of Chicago Press.

Adler, Emily Steir., (2008)
Invitation to Social Research,
Australia: Wadsworth Learning.

Anderson, T.W., (1958)
An Introduction to Multivariate Analysis,
New York: John Wiley & Sons.

Babbie, Earl., (2004)
The Practice of Social Research,
Canada: Thompson.

Barzun, J and Graff, Henry F., (1970)
The Modern Researcher (Rev. Ed.),
New York: Harcout Brace & World. Inc.

Berdie, Douglas R and Anderson, John F. , (1974)
Questionnaire: Design and Use,
Methuchen N.J: The Scarecrow Press Inc.

Bhandarkar, P. L.,   (2010)
Methodology and Techniques of Social Research,
New Delhi: Himalaya Publishing House.

Bhattacharya, Dipak kumar.,   (2003)
Research Methodology,
New Delhi: Excell Books.

Bhattacharya, Srinibas.,   (1972)
Psychometric and Behavioural Research,
New Delhi: Sterling Press.

Bordens, Kenneth S., (2011)
Research Design and Methods: A Process Approach,
New Delhi: Tata McGraw- Hill.

Bryman, Alan.,   (2008)
Social Research Methods,
New Delhi: Oxford University Press.

Chawla, Deepak R., (2011)
Research Methodology,
New Delhi: Vikas Publications.

Cochran, W.G., (1963)
Sampling Techniques (2ⁿᵈ ed.),
New York: John Wiley & Sons.

Cooley, William W and Lahnes, Paul R., (1971)
Multivariate Data Analysis,
New York: John Wiley & Sons.

Creswel, John W.,   (2009)
Research Design,
New Delhi: Sage Publications.

Dennis, Child.,   (1973)
The Essentials of Factor Analysis,
New York: Holt, Rinehart and Winstone.

Edmonds, Holly.,   (1999)
The Focus Group Research Handbook,
NTC, USA.

Festinger, Leon and Katz, Danial (Eds.), (1976)
Research Methods in Behavioural Sciences,
New Delhi: Amerind Publishing Co. Pvt. Ltd.
(4th Indian Reprint)

Fisher, R.A., (1958)
Statistical Methods for Research Workers (13rh ed.),
New York: Hafner Publishing Co.

Fox, James Harold.,   (1958)
Criteria of Good Research,
Phi Delta Kappa, Vol.39, March, 1958.

Freedman, P., (1960)
The Principles of Scientific Research,
New York: Pergamon Press.

Fruchter, Benjamin., (1954)
Introduction to Factor Analysis,
Princeton, N.J: D Van Nostrand.

Gibbons, J.D., (1971)
Nonparametric Statistical Inference,
Tokyo: McGraw-Hill Kogarkusha Ltd. International Student edition.

Ghose, R.N., (1982)
Scientific Methods and Social Research,
New Delhi: Sterling Publishers.

Gopal, M.H., (1965)
Research Reporting in Social Sciences,
Dharward: Karnataka University.

Gopal, M.H., (1964)
An Introduction to Research Procedure in Social Sciences,
Bombay: Asia Publishing House.

Gupta, Santhosh., (2001)
Research Methodology and Statistical Techniques,
New Delhi: Deep Deep Publications.

Harnett, Donald L and Murphy, James L.,   (1975)
Introductory Statistical Analysis,
Philippines: Addison-Wesley Publishing .

Hollander, Myles and Wolfe, Douglas A., (1973)
Nonparametric Statistical Methods,
New York: John Wiley & sons.

Hyman, Herbert H et.al., (1975)
Interview in Social Research,
Chicago: University of Chicago Press.

Johnson, Ellen.,   (1951)
The Research Report: A guide for the Beginner,
New York: Ronald Press

Kerlinger, Fred N.,   (1973)
Foundations of Behavioural Research (2nd ed.),
New York: Holt, Rinehart and Winston.

Kish, Leslie.,   (1965)
Survey Sampling,
New York: John Wiley & Sons.

Kothari C.R.,   (2007)
Research Methodology: Methods and Techniques,
                    (2nd Rev. Ed.)
New Delhi: New Age International (P) Ltd Publishers.

Krishnamoorthy, O.R.,   (2012)
Methodology of Research in Social Sciences,
New Delhi: Himalaya Publishing House.

Kumar, Ashok.,   (1997)
Social Research Methods,
New Delhi: Anmol Publications.

Kumar, Ranjit.,   (2011)
Research Methodology,
New Delhi: Sage Publications.

Lastrucci, Charles L.,   (1967)
The Scientific Approach: Basic Principles of Scientific Methods,
Cambridge, Mass: Schenkaman Publishing Co.

Lazarfeld, Paul F.,   (1950)
Evidence and Inference in Social Research,
(in David Lerher (Edr): Evidence and Inference
Glencoe: The Free Press.

Loseke, Donileen R., (2013)
Methodological Thinking,
New Delhi: Sage Publications.

Marannel, Gary M. (ed), (1974)
Scaling: A Source Book for Behavioural Scientists,
Chicago: Aldine.

Maxwell, Alebert E.,   (1961)
Analysing Quantitative Data,
New York: John Wiley & Sons.

Miller, Delbert C.,   (1977)
*Handbook of Research Design and Social Measurenment (3rd*
ed.),
New York: David Mckay Comany Inc.

Mohankumar, P.S., (1998)
A Handbook on Research Methodology,
Kudevechoor: Right Publications.

Murray, Rowens., (2006)
How to Write a Thesis,
New Delhi: Tata McGraw-Hill.

Nakkiran, S.,   (2001)
Research Methods in Social Sciences,
Mumbai: Himalaya Publications.

Neuman, Lawrence W.,   (2006)
Social Research Methods: Quantitative and Qualitative
Approaches,
New Delhi: Pearson.

Odum, H.W and Jocher, Katherine., (1929)
An Introduction to Social Research,
New York: Henry Holt and Co.

O'Leary, Zina., (2004)
The Essential Guide to Doing Research,
New Delhi: Vistaar Publications.

Popper, Karl R.,   (1959)
The Logic of Scientific Discovery,
New York: Basic Books.

Ramachandran P., (1971)
Training in Research Methodology in
Social Sciences in India,
New Delhi: ICSSR.

Sharma, B.A.V et. al.,   (1983)
Research Methods in Social Sciences,
New Delhi: Sterling Publishers.

Singh, Kultar.,   (2007)
Quantitative Social Research Methods,,
New Delhi: Sage Publications.

Singh Yogendra Kumar.,   (2006)
Fundamentals of Research Methodology and Statistics,
New Delhi: New Age International.

Tandon, B. C.,   (1979)
Research Methodology in Social Sciences,
Allahabad: Chaitanya Publishing House.

Thakur, Devendra., (1998)
Research Methodology in Social Sciences,
New Delhi: Deep Deep Publications.

Thanulingam, N., (2001)
Research Methodology,
New Delhi: Himalaya Publications.

Thurstone, L.L., (1959)
The Measurement of Values,
Chicago: University of Chicago Press.

Togerson, W., (1958)
Theory and Methods of Scaling,
New York: John Wiley & Sons.

Whitney, F. L., (1950)
The Elements of Research (3rd ed.),
New York: Prentice-Hall.

Wilkinson, T. S., (2002)
Methodology and Techniques of Social Research,
New Delhi: Himalaya Publications.

Willemson, Eleanor Walker., (1974)
Understanding statistical Reasoning,
San Francisco: W.H. Freeman and Company.

Young, Pauline V., (1960)
Scientific Social Surveys and Research (3rd ed.),
New York: Prentice-Hall.

Appendix – I

Temporal Sequence of the Variables

Figure-1.

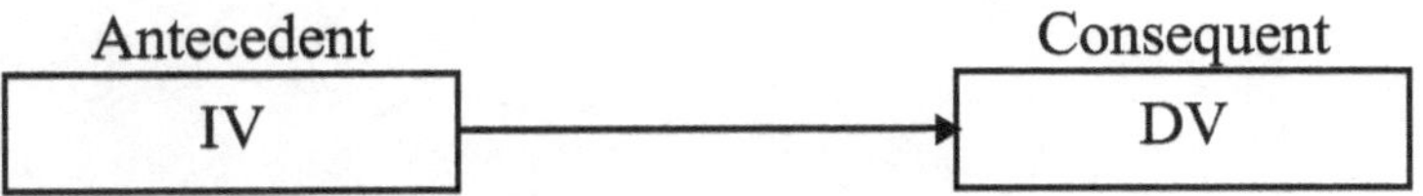

Note. In classical laboratory experiment, all extraneous variables are eliminated/neutralize/controlled by the experimental design. There are no moderating/mediating/ intervening variables in such designs.

Figure-2.

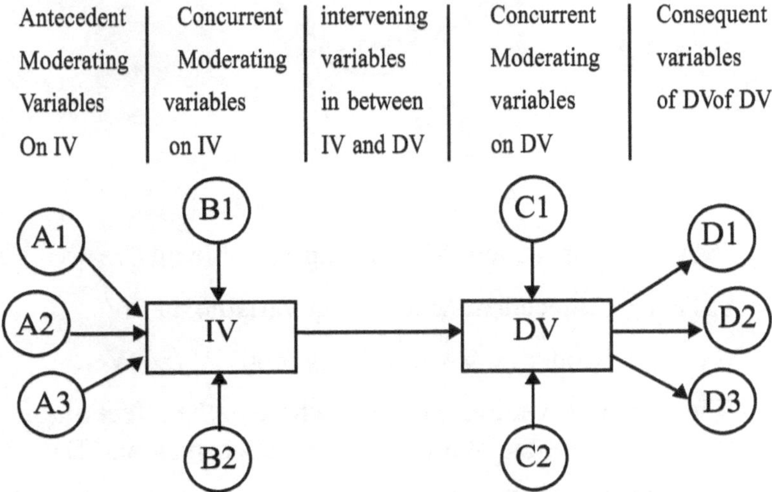

A 1,2,3,.....etc : Antecedent moderating variables on IV

B 1,2,3,.....etc : Concurrent moderating variables on IV

C1,2,3, ...etc : Concurrent moderating variables on DV

D 1,2,3, ...etc : Consequent Variables of DV (To be a supplementary study as the original DV is likely to be IV to the consequent variables which now become the new DV.

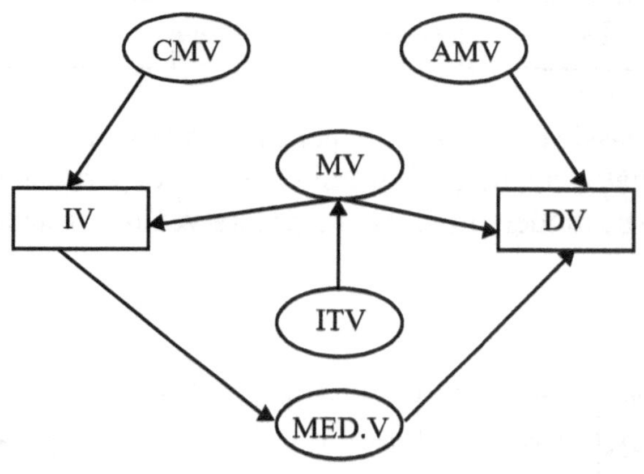

Note :

CMV   : Consequent Moderating Variable on IV

AMV   : Antecedent Modertaing Variable on DV

MV   : Moderating Variables on both IV & DV

ITV   : Intervening Variables where in the effect of the presence of a variable in between IV and DV.

MEDV : Mediating Variables : (IV on MEDV and MEDV on DV) in between IV and DV. The direction IV→ Med.V. → DV

Appendix- II

Multiple Independent Variables (IV)
and Dependent Variables (DVs).

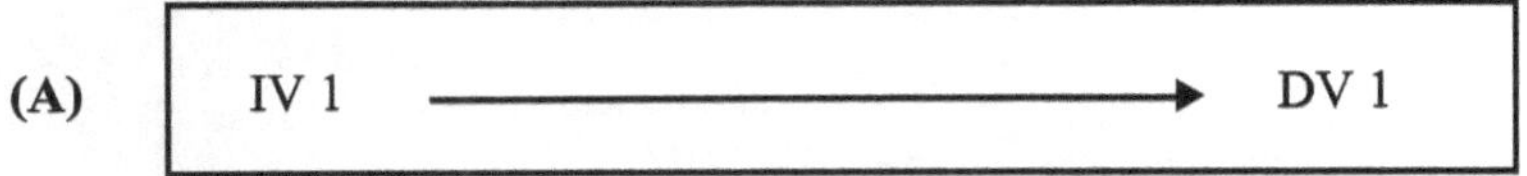

Only one IV and one DV as in the classical laboratory experimental design.

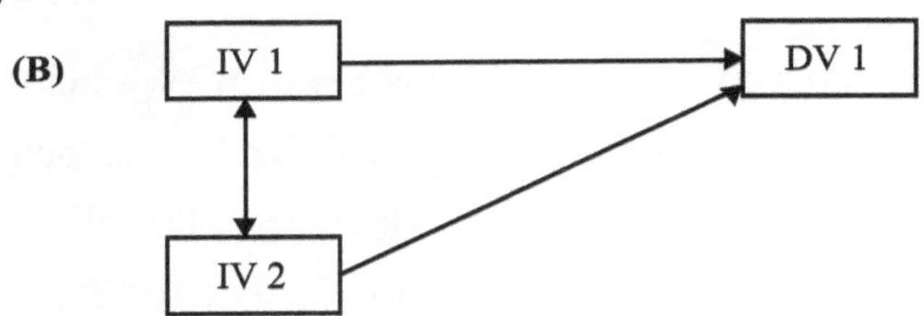

Note:

1. If IV 2 has significant correlation with IV 1, then IV 2 is only a sub-variable (moderating variable) of IV 1.
2. If IV 2 has no significant association with DV1, then IV2 is either irrelevant or it act as a moderating variable to IV1 or DV1.

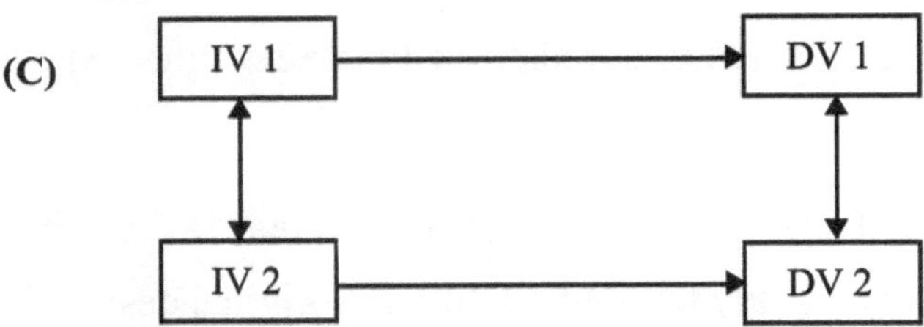

Note:

1. If there is not association between IV1 and IV2 and also DV1 and DV2, then they are two independent studies. If there is any association between IV1 and IV2, then IV2 is only a Moderating Variable on IV 1. Similarly if there is association between DV1 and DV2, then DV2 is a moderation Variable to DV1.

(D) 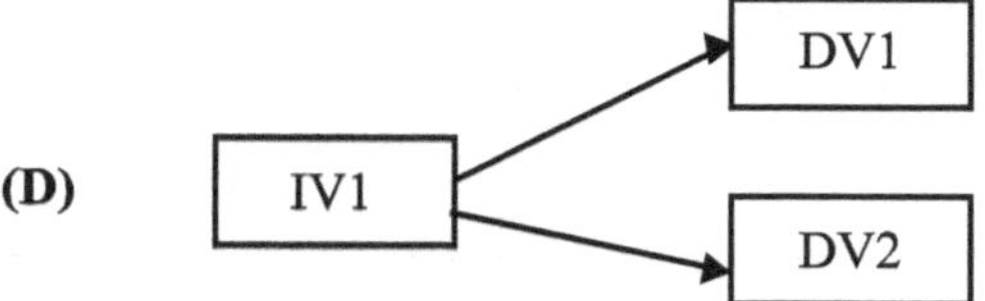

Note:

1. If there is no significant association between DV1 and DV2, but significant association between IV 1 and DV2, then they are two independent studies with the same IV1.

2. If there is signficant association between DV1 and DV2, then DV2 is only a Moderating Variable to DV1.

It is possible to have several IVs and DVs in Field experiments as in agriculture wherein many different studies are undertaken simultaneously with different blocks/plots for variations and controls of extraneous variables. Note that they are different studies undertaken at the same time, but not in temporal sequence.

The consequent variables of the original DV constitute a supplementary study without diluting the original design. In that supplementary study the consequent variable of the original study becomes the DV and the original DV becomes the IV with several other variables affecting both the IV and DV.

Appendix - III

Venn Diagrams of the Four Propositions and conversion or immediate inferences from such propositions

Figure- 1

Proposition 'A': Universal positive statement.
"All Crows are Black"

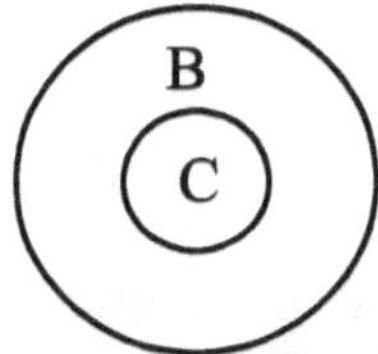

The immediate inference from the given statement " All Crows are Black" is that "Some Blacks are Crows" and not " All Blacks are Crows"

Figure-2

Proposition 'E': Universal negative statement
"No Crows are Black"

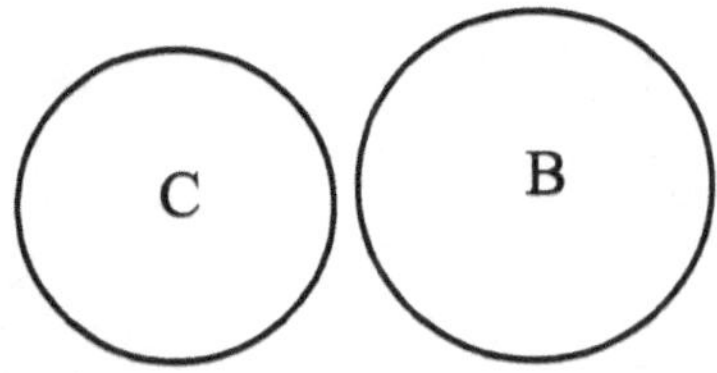

Immediate inference: "No Blacks are Crows"

Figure -3

Proposition 'I': Particular positive statement
"Some Crows are Black"

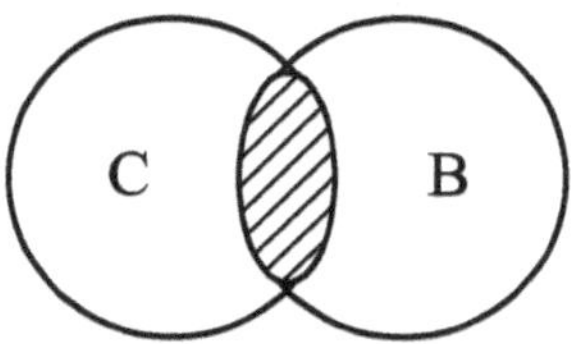

In this figure, the shaded portion is the common overlapping area which conveys the meaning that "Some Crows are Black" and the immediate inference is "Some Blacks are Crows".

Figure- 4

Proposition 'O': Particular negative statement.
"Some Crows are not Black"

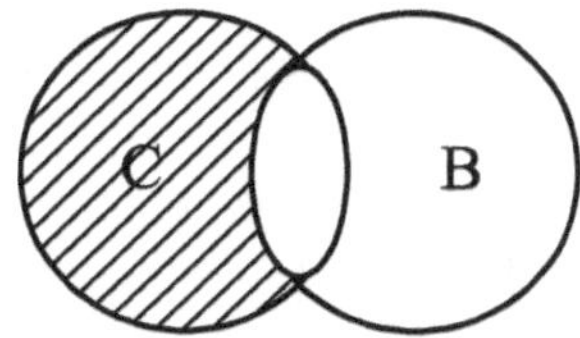

The shaded portion conveys the meaning that "Some Crows are not Black". An immediate inference is not possible from the statement "Some Crows are not Black" on the following reasons: The subject term 'Crows' is undistributed and the predicate term 'not Black' is distributed. When you convert the statement as "Some Blacks are not Crows", the predicate term 'not Crows' gets distributed which is undistributed in the original statement— a fallacy similar to the fallacy of illicit major. No conversion is possible in particular negative statements.

Appendix- IV

SQUARE OF LOGICAL OPPOSITION AMONG THE FOUR BASIC PROPOSITIONS

'A' proposition

'E'P Proposition

All men are mortal

No men are mortal

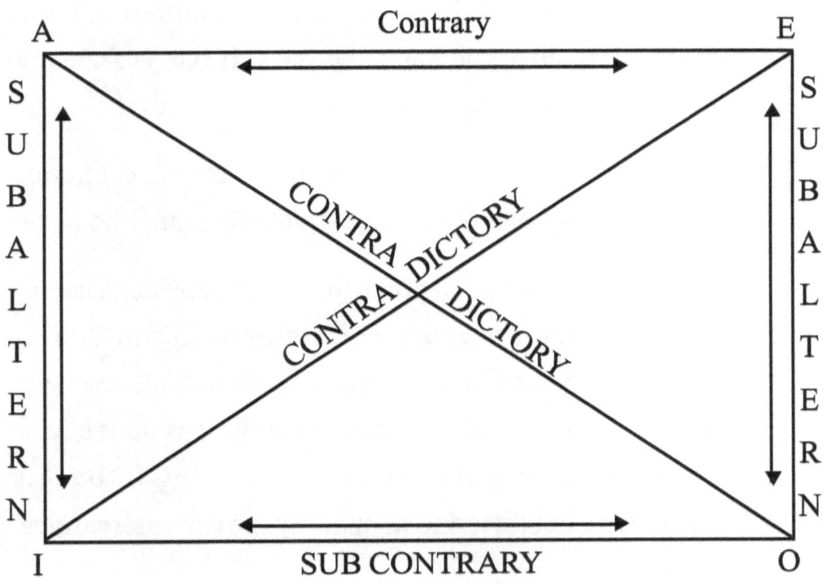

'I' Proposition
Some men are mortal

'O' Proposition
Some men are not mortal

1.   Contradictories: 'A' and 'O' propositions are contradictories; and so is the case with 'E' and 'I' propositions. In contradictory statements, both cannot be true and both cannot be false. If one is true, the other one has to be false; if one is false, the other one has to be true.

2.   Contraries: 'A' and 'E' propositions are contraries. If one is true, the other one has to be false. If one is false, the other one is doubtful. But, both can be false.

3.   Sub-contraries: 'I' and 'O' propositions are sub-contraries. Both propositions can be true, but both cannot be false.

4.   Sub-alterns : 'A' and 'I' propositions. Propositions having the same subject and predicate agreeing in quality (positive), but differing in quantity are sub-alterns (sub-alternatives). 'E' and 'O' propositions. Propositions having the same subject and predicate agreeing in quality (negative), but differing in quantity are sub-alternatives.

If the universal ('A' or 'E') is true, the particular ('I' or "O') is also true, but if the particular is true, the universal is doubtful. If the universal is false, the particular is doubtful. If the particular is false, the universal is also false.

Appendix-V
Sample size to a given population

Population Size	Sample Size Confidence=95% Margin of error		Sample Size Confidence=99% Margin of error	
	5%	3.5%	5%	3.5%
10	10	10	10	10
50	44	47	47	48
100	80	89	87	93
500	217	306	285	365
1000	278	440	399	575
5000	357	678	586	1066
10,000	370	727	622	1193
50,000	381	772	655	1318
1,00,000	383	778	659	1336
10,00,000	384	783	663	1352
25,00,000	384	784	663	1353
100,00,000	384	784	663	1354

Source: www.research-advisors.com tools/sample size.htm

Date of reference: 20th August, 2014.
(copy right: The research Advisors,2005.)

SUBJECT INDEX

Subject Index.

Page No.

A

'A' Proposition
Abductive Logic 53
Acceptance / Rejection of Hypothesis
Acceptance / Rejection of Null Hypothesis
Accuracy 67
Action Research 77
Alpha error 77
Alternative Hypothesis 78
Amount 83
Analayses of data
Analytical Research 85
ANOCOVA 77
ANOVA 77
Antecedent 90
Antecedent conditons
Antecedent Variables 78
APA 78
Appendices 75
Applied Research 78
Approaches 89
Area Sampling 78
Argument 39
Art of reviewing 26
Association 29
Assumptions 68
Attributes 68
Availability of data 32

B

Beta error   78
Bibliography   78
Binary digits   78
Bipolar   78

C

Canonical Analysis   79
Canonical Correlation   79
Case Studies   79
Categorical Attributes   79
Categorical Satetements
Categorical Variables   79
Causal analysis   79
Caustive Principles   79
Cause-effect relationship   79
Central Limit Theorem   79
Chi-square80
Chroneback's Alpha   80
Clarity
Classification   84
Classificatory Research   10
Clinical Research   80
Cluster analysis   80
Cluster Sampling   80
Coding   41
Completely Random Design   80
Composite Standard Method   81
Concepts   102
Conceptual   11
Conclusions   9
Concomitant Variations   81
Concurrent Validity   81
Concurrent Variables   81
Conditional Logic/Reasoning   81
Confidence Level   81

Confounding relations 81
Confounding Variables 81
Connotation 81
Consequent Variable 81
Consolidated References
Construct 82
Construct Validity 82
Content Analysis 82
Content Oriented Research 82
Content Validity 82
Continuous Series 82
Contradictory Statements 83
Contracry Statements 83
Contributions to academics
Controlled Variables 77
Convenient Sampling 83
Conversation of quality into quantity
Conversion of quantitative variations into categorical attributes
Conversions 61
Copula 83
Correlation 83
Correlation Analysis 83
Correlative Research 83
Covariance 83
Covariant relations
Co-variations 101
Criterion related validity 83
Cross Sectional Research 84
Cross Tabulation 84
Cumulative Scale 84

D

Data 84
Data Analyses 84
Data collection 84
Data Distribution 89
Data Inferences 84

Data Interpretations 84
Data Processing 68
Deductive Logic 77
Deductive Process 84
Deductive Reasoning 47
Deliberate Sampling 61
Denotation 85
Dependent Variable (DV) 35
Descriptive Research 85
Descriptive Statistics 85
Descriptive Survey research
Descriptive Vs Analaytical Research
Diagnostic Research 85
Differences 85
Differential Scale 85
Difficulty Level 86
Dimensions 37
Discrete Numbers 41
Discrete Variables 86
Discrimination Index 86
Discriminative Values
Distributed Denotation 86
Distribution free data 66
Distribution free statistics 87
Distribution of Data 87
Distribution of the predicate term 61
Distribution of the subject term 61
Distribution pattern 66
Diversities 81
Dysfunctional 14

E

'E' Proposition 49
Effect Variable
Empirical 9
Empirical Hypothesis testing type Research

Empirical Research   20
Equivalent Form Method   87
Evaluative Research   88
Ex post facto Research   88
Experimental Design   93
Experimental Group   22
Experimental Research   20
Experimental Vs Control Group   87
Explanatory Research   88
Extraneous Variables   88

F

Factor Analysis   88
Factorial Design   88
Fallacies of reasoning :
accepting both contradictories
accepting the indeterminate as True or False
Ad hominem   64
Ad ignoratium   65
Affirmation of the antecedent by the
affirmation of the consequent
Ambiguous Middle   61
Appeal to non issues   65
False cause (post hoc ergo propter hoc)   64
Gamblers' fallacy   65
Generalizations from exceptions   65
Ignoring the common cause   64
Ignoring the intermediate cause
Illicit Major   89
Illicit Minor   89
Incomparable Analogies   64
Limited Sample   63
Making two wrongs as right
More than three terms
Petition principia

Poisoning the well 64
Questionable cause 64
Red herring 64
Relativistic / subjective experience
Special pleading 64
The middle ground 64
The straw man 64
Two Negative Propositions 89
Two Particular Propositions 89
Undistributed Middle 89
Verbal labelling 64
Falsity of a proposition / statement
Field Observations / Research
Field work 74
Fine discrimination 67
Finite Population 68
Fundamental Research 89

G

Generalizations 89
Guttman's Cumulative Type Scale / Scalogram 90

H

Harvard System of giving references 90
Heterogeneity 109
Hierarchical levels in research
Historical Research 90
Homogeneity 89
H-test 90
Hypothesis (H1)
Hypothesis testing research 90
Hypothetico - deductive logic 90

I

'I' Proposition 91
Identification of a research topic
Identification of variables 22

Ideographic 90
Immediate Inference 90
Independent Variable (IV) 90
Inductive Logic 90
Inductive Process 90
Inductive Reasoning 109
Inferences 124
Inferential Statistics 66
Infinite Population 68
Information gap in research
Instruments 91
Intangible qualitative attributes 41
Intellectual honesty 30
Interaction Effect 91
Interactive variations
Interconnectedness of variables
Inter-judge variations
Internal Consistency
Interpersonal relations
Interpretations and discussions
Inter-quartile range
Interval Scale 102
Intervening variables 120
Interview 23
Item analysis 43

J

Joint Method of Agreement and Difference 57
Judgement Sampling

K

Kendal's coefficient of correlation 92
Known differentiated groups
Kruskal - Wallis H - test
Kurtosis 92

L

Laboratory Research 21
Latent structure analysis 93
Latin square design 93
Law of comparative judgement 93
Leptokurtic 93
Library Research 94
Likert's Summated type Scale 94
Literature Support
Logic 94
Logic of arriving at generalizations
Logic of deriving conclusions 17
Logic of establishing cause - effect relations
Longitudinal Research 94

M

Major Premise 94
MANACOVA 94
Management of Research
Mann-Whitney U-test 94
MANOVA 94
Mathematical formula 96
Mathematical Models 98
Maximum Likelihood
Mean 111
Measurement 41
Measurement in Social Sciences
Measurement of Attitudes
Measurement of Relationships 95
Measurement Scales 41
Measures of Association 95
Measures of Central Tendencies 95
Measures of Differences 95
Measures of Dispersions 95
Measuring test / instruments
Median 94

Mediate Inference

Mediating Variables 94

Mesokurtic 95

Method of Agreement 95

Method of Concomitant Variations 95

Method of Difference 95

Method of giving references 15

Method of Residue 58

Method Vs Methodology

Methodology 59

Methods

Middle Term 61

Minor Premise 96

Mode 96

Model 96

Moderating Variables 96

Modification of the title

Multiple Analysis of Variance 97

Multiple Correlations 97

Multiple Variables 97

Multi-regression Analysis

Multivariate Analsysis 97

N

Necessary and sufficient cause 57

Necessary cause

Negative Proposition / statement

Nominal Scale 97

Nomothetic 97

Nonparametric Statistics 97

Normal Probability Distribution 98

Null Hypothesis (HO) 98

O

'O' Proposition   98
Objectives   98
Observational Research
Operational Defintion   98
Ordinal Scale   98
Other variables   82
Outliers   98

P

Parametric Statistics   98
Partial Correlation   98
Pariticipative Observations   99
Particular Negative Proposition   99
Particular Positive Proposition   99
Particular Proposition   99
Path Analysis Technique   99
Pearson Coefficient Correlation   99
Phenomenon   109
Phenomenon under observation
Philosophy   99
Pilot Study   99
Plagiarism   100
Population   100
Positive Proposition   100
Practical Applications
Predicate of the Proposition   100
Prediction   100
Premises   100
Presentation of the Thesis   17
Primary data / source   94
Principles of Causation   56
Principles of Reasoning

Probability Theory 100
Problem 100
Problem Oriented Research 100
Process Vs Outcome
Proposition 101
Pure Research 20

Q

Qualitative 101
Qualitative Attributes 34
Qualitative Vs Quantitative Research 101
Quality of a Thesis
Quantification 101
Quantification and Measurement 101
Quantitative 101
Quantitative variations 111
Quartile Deviation 101
Questionnaire 101
Quota Sampling 101

R

Random Sampling method 101
Range 102
Rating Scale 108
Ratio Scale 102
Realistic and Pragmatic
Recommendations 60
Redesing the research design
Reference in the Text 26
References 102
Regression Analysis 102
Reliability 102
Research
Research Goals
Research Design 102

Research Ethics 102
Research Process 102
Research Title 16
Research Topic 16
Review of Literature
Risk and Uncertainity

S

Sample 102
Sample Design 103
Sample Frame 103
Sample of the Population 102
Sample Size 103
Sampling Design 103
Sampling Error 104
Sampling Methods 104
Sampling Units 104
Scales of Measurements 104
Scaling / Scale construction Methods 104
Scalogram 104
Schedule 104
Scholarship part of the Research 105
Scope of a Research Study
Search in Research
Secondary Data 18
Secondary Source References
Selection of Items / Statements 101
Selection of the target population 67
Self Consistency 102
Sense of Direction 14
Sequential Sampling 105
Sign Test 105
Significance Levels 105
Similarities 105
Similarities and Differences 19

Skewness 106
Social Sciences 106
Sources of errors 106
Spearman's Rank Order Correlation 106
Specificity of Variables
Split - half Method of Reliability
SPSS
Standard Deviation 106
Standard Error 106
Standardization
Standards
Statement 106
Statement of a Problem
Statement Vs Hypothesis
Statements - Categorical
Statements - Conditional
Statistical Analyses
Stastical Methods
Statistics 106
Statistics for Research 66
Statistics for Research in Social Sciences 66
Stratified random sampling method 108
Structural Equation Modelling (SEM) 107
Structuring the Research Work/report
Subaltern statements 107
Sub-contrary Statements 107
Subject of Research
Subject of the Proposition 107
Sub-sample for the Pilot Study
Sub-samples
Sub-variables
Sufficient Cause
Summated Scale
Supplementary Study

Survey type descriptive research
Syllogistic Reasoning
Systematic Random sampling

T

Target Population   108
Techniques   108
Temporal Sequence of Variables
Tentative Research Design
Test-Retest Reliability Method   108
Tests
Tests of Significance
Theoretical Frame work
Theoretical Research   109
Theoretical Significance
Theories of Causation
Theory   109
Thesis Format
Thurstone's Scale   109
Time
Time Constraints
Time Series
Tools and Instruments   109
Tools and Methods
Tools for data collection
Trial and Error Method
Truthfulness of a proposition   109
t-test   109
Type I error   109
Type II error   109

U

Uncertainty   109
Undistributed Middle Term   89
Undistriubuted Terms   89

Unethical practice
Unfamiliar
Uniformity
Unipolar Scale
Unity
Universal Negative Propositions
Universal Positive Propositions
Universe
Unstructured
Use of et... al in references
Use of Judges
U-test   110

V

Validity of tests / instruments
Validity of Conclusions
Values   111
Variables   111
Varimax Rotation   111

W

Wilcoxon - Mann - Whitney test

X

X, the assumed cause of Y
X-axis

Y

Y, the phenomenon under observations
Y = f(x)

Z

Z-score
Z-test

www.ingramcontent.com/pod-product-compliance
Lightning Source LLC
Chambersburg PA
CBHW031229250726
48655CB00005B/1874